I0824653

VIEW FROM THE EAST WING

ALSO BY JILL BIDEN

Where the Light Enters

Willow the White House Cat

Joey: The Story of Joe Biden

Don't Forget, God Bless Our Troops

VIEW FROM THE EAST WING

A MEMOIR

JILL BIDEN

GALLERY BOOKS

New York Amsterdam/Antwerp London
Toronto Sydney/Melbourne New Delhi

Gallery Books
An Imprint of Simon & Schuster, LLC
1230 Avenue of the Americas
New York, NY 10020

Photograph credits on page 273

First Gallery Books hardcover edition June 2026

GALLERY BOOKS and colophon are registered trademarks of Simon & Schuster, LLC

Interior design by Jaime Putorti

Manufactured in the United States of America

10 9 8 7 6 5 4 3 2 1

Library of Congress Control Number: 2026937974

ISBN 978-1-6682-2288-1
ISBN 978-1-6682-2290-4 (ebook)

To my daughter, Ashley;

My granddaughters Naomi, Finnegan, Maisy, and Natalie—

And to all women finding their way forward.

May you embrace your independence and stay true to yourself.

Tell me, what is it you plan to do
with your one wild and precious life?
—Mary Oliver, "The Summer Day"

VIEW FROM THE EAST WING

PROLOGUE

"Once you lose a child, nothing can hurt you."

This was the spontaneous answer I gave at a 2019 fundraising event when I was asked how our family was going to handle the vitriol and accusations that were being hurled at us. Joe and I knew the campaign wasn't going to be easy. We had witnessed the tactics of his opponent before. Yes, our family was still shattered, but we were resilient. It was the truest statement I could make in response, and uncharacteristically personal.

In 2015, our son Beau died from brain cancer at age forty-six. At the time, Joe and I were living at the vice president's residence in Washington, DC. For two years, we had been going from hospital to hospital, doctor to doctor, trying to cure him. Christiana Hospital in Delaware, Jefferson and U. Penn in Philadelphia, MD Anderson in Houston, trials, medicines, diets—there were no answers. Joe and I served as Vice President and Second Lady, and stole precious hours whenever we could to be with Beau. We went home to Delaware nearly every weekend to be together.

Few knew Beau was dying. For his sake and that of his wife, Hallie, and for their two small children, we couldn't bear the thought of public discussion around his illness. Those months I felt like I was walking through water, barely pushing through, trying to breathe, not believing it was possible that he would die. Beau was special. Really, ask anyone who knew him—friends or enemies. I could not imagine God taking him, but He did. I had trouble believing in a higher power or a just universe that would let Beau suffer, much less leave his children fatherless. My entire family was out of control, spinning with grief. Joe and I numbly put one foot in front of the other. We kept moving.

Later, throughout the years we spent in the White House, I felt steeled against whatever happened. Whenever things got really bad—as they did—I knew that I'd been through much worse.

The saving grace was that we had our health. Every single day, I remembered to give thanks in my morning prayers for our health. Then I asked for strength to help my family endure whatever challenges we might face. Joe and I could always find a way to cope through the bad times by saying to each other, "We still have our health. Our children and grandchildren are healthy."

So it came as a surprise to me when, just four months after we left office, we found out that Joe had an aggressive form of prostate cancer that had metastasized to his bones. Prostate cancer was one thing, but the metastasis turned it into something infinitely worse. Hormone therapy would always be part of his life. Daily meds would always be needed to keep cancer's progression at bay. What were the side effects going to be? How much of what happened in the future would be a result of medication versus aging? It was impossible to know. And yet, after Beau's death, I knew there was nothing Joe and I couldn't handle together. Nothing.

CHAPTER 1

Early in the summer of 2025, it was just Joe and me at the place I loved best—sitting on the beach in Delaware watching the waves. We were chatting the way we have for almost fifty years now—about how the kids seemed, what we should have for dinner. We'd been out of the White House for several months, and we were finally beginning to feel some distance from the constant noise of the presidency.

Looking at Joe, I could still see in him the handsome, slightly mischievous man with whom I'd gone on a blind date in 1975. By that time, Joe had already experienced deep grief, having lost his first wife, Neilia, and year-old daughter, Naomi, in a 1972 car crash that also injured their two young sons, Beau and Hunter. Together, Joe and I raised the boys, and in 1981, we had a daughter, Ashley. I became a high school teacher, earned my EdD, and found my calling as a community college English professor—a job I kept even when we lived in the White House. In the wake of losing Beau to cancer, we'd almost lost Hunter to addiction. We'd become grandparents several times over—and recently great-grandparents to our sweet little boy Willie.

Joe's presidency was unprecedented in so many ways. He was sworn in with the city shrouded in barbed wire because the prior president's refusal to concede had caused the violent January 6 insurrection. The pandemic was still raging. On January 20, 2021, the date of Joe's inauguration, there were 4,409 COVID-19 deaths reported in the US—just in one day. People were terrified of catching it themselves or losing a loved one. We were a nation in pain: Grief. Isolation. Mental health crises.

The pandemic had cost America ten million jobs; whole industries were collapsing. Schools were closed, leaving parents to manage children and lessons online. The post–9/11 forever wars had cost America thousands of lives. After the death of George Floyd, political and racial tensions had reached historic levels; it felt as though trust in government and in one another was at an all-time low. An impossible situation, but one I believed Joe was uniquely qualified to handle because of his decades of experience reaching across the aisle and working to find compromise, and because of his integrity, innate decency, boundless compassion, and steady hand.

Each First Lady has approached the role in her own way. I vowed to make the most of my platform, particularly when it came to getting COVID under control, supporting military families and community colleges (as I had for eight years as Second Lady), promoting cancer research, and advocating for women's health. Still, I was a reluctant participant in politics. Growing up in a middle-class home in Willow Grove, Pennsylvania, the daughter of a World War II veteran, the oldest of five girls, I was happiest off on my own in the corner with a stack of books.

As the sun beat down that day on the Delaware beach, I marveled at the twists of fate that had brought us onto the global stage. Joe's deep knowledge of foreign policy, thanks to his thirty-six years in the Senate, made him the right vice presidential candidate to join Barack

Obama in the historic 2008 election. Then there was Joe's campaign in 2020, which began with a tough primary but ended with a sweet victory . . .

My reverie was interrupted by the sight of a figure walking toward Joe and me through the sand. This wasn't surprising—people come up to us all the time. They want to talk about politics or just say hi. We're always up for it. Well, Joe is always up for it. I send him to the store, and he returns three hours later, having taken two dozen selfies and called somebody's mother to sing her "Happy Birthday." I'm an introvert, so I do my best. When Joe and I stand together onstage, I often give him a little squeeze to signal, *Okay, wrap it up. People want to go home.* Sometimes when I do that, he tells the crowd, "Jill just pinched me because she thinks I'm going on too long!"

That's Joe Biden, a politician in the best sense of the word—shaking everybody's hands, listening intently as they share their concerns and their hopes and the latest news of their college sports teams. Joe was that way as a senator, as vice president, and as president. People flock to him for handshakes and hugs, and he is delighted by all of it. If he's talking to you, he never has a more important place to be—even when he does have a more important place to be. So I expected this beach conversation would likely go on for a while.

The woman put both her hands on Joe's chair, leaned into him, and said, "I'm a doctor. How did your doctor not pick up this cancer diagnosis earlier?"

Well, that was not the "hello" I'd expected, though it was a fair question, one that I had struggled with myself. Two months earlier, we'd been shocked to discover, along with the rest of the world, that Joe had stage IV prostate cancer that had metastasized to his bones. Ever since his surprise late-stage cancer diagnosis, people had been offering well-wishes tinged with confusion—how was it possible no one caught it before it spread?

Joe, always the optimist, thanked the woman for her concern and said, "I have the best doctors. I'm going to get through this."

For my part, I didn't want to think about cancer just then. Joe and I had been enjoying a rare tranquil day. Once his cancer diagnosis was mentioned, his expression changed. Mine, too. I forced a smile. *Thank you for your care, Doctor*, I thought, *but I hope you'll understand this isn't the right time to discuss this. We're in our bathing suits, and we're trying to relax.*

So much about the past year has been a total shock. I've found myself asking again and again, *How did we end up here?*

As the novelist James Salter wrote, "There are stories one must tell and years when one must tell them." The time to discuss those four years in the White House—so much that I've avoided even letting myself think about—is now.

I'll begin with what would have been my answer to the concerned doctor on the beach and anyone else with the same question.

In the year before we left the White House, Joe began waking up repeatedly at night. This symptom, I knew, was common in men his age, and almost always caused by something benign. Joe never missed his annual physical—at his February 28, 2024, exam at Walter Reed Medical Center, his doctor proclaimed him "a healthy, active, robust 81-year-old male, who remains fit to successfully execute the duties of the Presidency"—and he had access to the best medical care available. Right there in the residence, there's a fully staffed twenty-four-hour doctor's office. You stop in because you have a headache, because your throat is sore, because you need your flu shot or COVID booster.

Knowing that Joe would prefer to speak about any urological issues with his male doctors rather than with his wife, I alerted one of them to make sure they knew. "He was up seven times last night," I said. "I'm worried about him."

Now that the doctors had been made aware of the issue, I trusted that Joe would be examined and treated. But as far as I could tell, the issue persisted. Even knowing this, I never imagined that the cause of this very common symptom of age would turn out to be cancer.

While it surely sounds old-fashioned that I spoke about the issue to the doctors rather than to Joe directly, it's always been the nature of our relationship that we've maintained a veil of discretion around personal health. When I went through menopause, I never spoke about it with him, even though I experienced two years of horrible insomnia, and when I did manage to fall asleep I was jolted awake by night sweats.

Back in Wilmington, I realized that Joe's symptoms had gotten worse, and I encouraged him to make an appointment with a urologist.

Joe went up to Thomas Jefferson University Hospital in Philadelphia for the appointment. At the very first examination, the doctor said, "There's something here. We need to find out what it is." He sent Joe for a biopsy May 15.

We got a call later that same day. The urologist told us that Joe had cancer, and he ordered various other tests to find out if the cancer had spread.

One of the questions we've been asked is why Joe hadn't had a recent prostate exam. That was a question I had, too. I've since learned that the American Urological Association doesn't recommend routine prostate-specific antigen (PSA) screening for men older than seventy. The thinking is that prostate cancer usually spreads more slowly in older men. Cancer at that age doesn't tend to affect life expectancy, which for men in the US is about seventy-six. Sometimes the risk of performing a biopsy in an older man can outweigh the benefits.

Due to a high PSA, Joe's cancer appeared to be advanced. We still had hope, though, that the cancer was localized to his prostate. Joe went for a PET scan, also at Jefferson Hospital, on May 16. We waited for the scan results in an exam room that was the size of a closet. It had a curtain, not a door. Joe was in the exam chair, and I was sitting on a chair they'd brought in for me.

The results didn't take long, about half an hour. The doctor opened the curtain. As soon as I saw her face, I knew.

"I'm sorry," she said. "Oh, I'm so sorry." She wouldn't stop saying "I'm sorry."

Stage IV. It had spread to his bones.

Prostate cancer is very common—one in eight men receive the diagnosis in their lifetime, and it is highly treatable when found early. So many men have notably had it and treated it successfully—John Kerry, Robert De Niro, Ben Stiller, Colin Powell, Warren Buffett . . . Yet, in all the cases I knew about, they'd caught it earlier; it hadn't spread to their bones.

I walked out of that closet of a room, past the Secret Service.

Breathe, I kept repeating to myself as I headed to the ladies' room to compose myself before I faced anyone.

Then the questions began—starting with what course of treatment would be best. We had to act fast. We needed a plan. Joe could do radiation and hormone therapy. Thanks to that regimen, he would have every hope of many more years left. His doctors said that it was unlikely the cancer would kill him; he would likely live out his natural life.

Breathe.

The press statement went out May 18. Joe's staff, the younger staffers in particular, were devastated. But we couldn't dwell in the grief because we were put immediately on the defensive, accused of having hidden his illness. The question became: How was it possible that the president of the United States, the most powerful man in the world, a man who has a medical team—not just a doctor, a *medical team*—around him twenty-four hours a day could wind up with cancer so advanced? Joe couldn't stub his toe without ten people wanting to run at him waving bales of gauze. You put the president in bubble wrap, and he ends up with stage IV prostate cancer? It made no sense.

Truly, I did not know what to say to people who were baffled like that doctor on the beach. I felt the same way. I was stunned. And yet, I didn't want to waste too much energy looking back and asking how this could have happened. We had no time to lose. He had to get started on treatment. Joe went in for a bone density test on May 21, and the next day he began hormone therapy. The hormone pills can cause serious side effects, particularly fatigue and moodiness. That has been true for Joe.

As anyone who's ever loved someone through a major illness knows—and I went through it with both my parents, and both Joe's parents, and, most excruciatingly, with Beau—you live in a world of questions: *What time is the physical therapist coming? Did he take his medicine? What did he have for breakfast? How much water is he drinking? He didn't sleep well last night—do I need to call the doctor?*

Worry becomes your constant companion.

Since 2009, as Second and First Lady, whenever I traveled across America, I saw the endurance of what I consider core American values: truth, loyalty, faith, community, service. Republican and Democrat families might disagree on the economy or social issues, but they share a love of country and a respect for the right to disagree.

While Joe was in office, I think he and I both erred on the side of silence, dignity, and letting news cycles run their course. Others might react to every slight, seize every opportunity to spin something to their advantage. We would stay out of the fray, play by the rules, ignore the ludicrous attacks, and assume that people would discern the truth. I preferred the path of discretion. I think many English teachers would opt to spend their free time reading rather than talking, and that is true of me. I'm from an era and a family in which we didn't speak openly about issues like mental health, drugs, sex, or anything uncomfortable.

When I hear some of the things that have been said of us, I find it baffling that anyone could believe them. I've been accused of either having been too involved in Joe's presidency or too hands-off. In the former scenario, I was some sort of puppet master; in the latter, it was my job to tell Joe not to run for president in 2024, or to drop out of the race sooner.

On the campaign trail for Joe when he was running for president way back in July 1987, I stood at a podium in Iowa and spoke to the question of who a First Lady should be. What did I know then? I was a senator's wife with three kids ranging in age from first grade to college, teaching high school English, wearing my favorite navy-and-white shoulder-padded suit because it made me feel confident. But the answer I gave wasn't too far from what I would say now:

> There is one objective—and that is to make Americans feel proud of their First Lady and to feel that in some way she is a reflection of their lives and their values. My own personal view is that the First Lady should respond to the concerns and the interests of today's American women. Women who are mothers, who are spouses, and who are wage earners. Women who are struggling to balance all three roles. And I think they would identify with a First Lady who is also trying to balance those three roles.

Many years later, I actually found myself balancing those roles as First Lady, and it was the honor of my life. I'm full of gratitude for the opportunity I was given to play a part in the country's history, even if my call to the office came under circumstances I never anticipated.

What I think I brought to my role as First Lady is the same thing I bring to my friendships and my family: the values I grew up with. I don't have any illusions about how tough life is, or how complicated human nature is. I've had an incredible life. Still, I think most of what's consumed me is universal to all women—how to balance work, family, my place in the community, my obligations to myself. I still believe that service is the highest calling, that small acts of kindness matter, and that deep down we are more alike than different. One of my favorite songs is Luke Bryan's "Most People Are Good." Even with all the evidence I've seen to the contrary, that's something I still believe, too.

The Danish philosopher Søren Kierkegaard said, "Life can only be understood backwards, but it must be lived forwards." I've been pushing forward so relentlessly that only now can I stop to make sense of everything. It's finally come time to sort through all that's happened—for my own understanding, and for the sake of history.

CHAPTER 2

After Joe left the vice presidency in 2017, we led more or less private lives, splitting our time between Delaware and the DC area, where we'd rented a house on Chain Bridge Road in McLean, Virginia. We continued our advocacy and established the Biden Foundation and the Biden Cancer Initiative, and I was board chair of Save the Children. I kept teaching English two days a week at Northern Virginia Community College (NOVA), as I had since 2009.

And yet, ever since the "Unite the Right" rally in Charlottesville in August 2017, where white supremacists and neo-Nazis brazenly chanted racist and anti-Semitic slogans, Joe had been preoccupied by doing whatever he could to help heal the divisions so brutally on display there. If he could bring the country together, shouldn't he? Everywhere I went, I heard people crying out for leadership. "You have to run!" people called to Joe on the street.

Were we ready to return to public life?

The choice felt heavy. Joe had always wanted to be president, but he'd begun to wonder if his time had passed. If he ran, I knew there would be a cost to our family. I did not particularly want to invite scrutiny, especially at a time when the kids and grandkids had been through so much. Another question was Joe's age. He would be seventy-eight when he took the oath of office. There was a lot to think about.

At the December 5, 2018, funeral for George H. W. Bush, the Washington National Cathedral was overflowing with politicians, ambassadors, public officials, friends, and family. Joe and I arrived from our house in Virginia. In a single pew from left to right sat the Trumps, the Obamas, the Clintons, and the Carters. Per protocol, former vice presidents like Joe sat in the row behind them, so we were in the same row as Mike and Karen Pence, Dan and Marilyn Quayle, Al Gore, and Dick and Lynne Cheney.

At state funerals, the speeches by both Republicans and Democrats tend to be thoughtful, incisive, and humorous, capturing the deceased in very personal ways. The elder Bush's was no exception. One of my favorite senators, Wyoming Republican Alan Simpson, recalled, "In one dark period, I was feeling awful low and all my wounds were self-inflicted, all of them. And George called me early one morning—always early in the morning, country music playing in the background—and he said, 'Ah, I see the media is shooting you pretty full of holes.' Actually, he said it a bit more pungently than that. And he said, 'Why don't we go up to Camp David? You and Ann come over and we'll have a weekend together.' At that time, his popularity rating was 93 percent. Mine was .93 percent."

Bush let them be photographed together, and Simpson said, "George, I am not unmindful as to what you are doing. You are propping up your old wounded-duck pal. While you're at the top of your game, you reach out to me while I'm tangled in rich controversy and taking my lumps." Bush's reply: "Yep."

George H. W. Bush's son, former president George W. Bush, said, "At age ninety, George H. W. Bush parachuted out of an aircraft and landed on the grounds of St. Ann's by the Sea in Kennebunkport, Maine, the church where his mom was married and where he worshipped often. Mother liked to say he chose the location just in case the chute didn't open." He paired the joke with a touching observation that his father "recognized that serving others enriched the giver's soul." This was something Joe believed, too.

Jenna Bush Hager gave a reading from the book of Revelation, and on the way back to her seat from the pulpit, she gently touched her grandfather's casket—a moving gesture of respect and affection that brought tears to my eyes.

As the assembled dignitaries listened to the eulogies, I caught some of them glancing over at Joe. I knew what they were thinking: *Would he enter the race for president?*

"Let's go have lunch," I suggested as we came out of the cathedral.

"Okay," Joe said. His aide Richard drove us in our black Suburban the ten minutes to BlackSalt restaurant, one of our date-night staples. The timing felt right. I knew the presidency was on both our minds.

"Chardonnay, please," I said.

Joe said, "I'll have a Diet Coke."

Before we'd even looked at the menu, I said: "This is it, Joe. You have to make up your mind. Are you going to run or not?"

"Yes, I want to run," he told me, matter-of-factly.

At last, clarity.

"Okay," I said. I would have responded the same way if he'd said he was going to quit politics.

The waiter came back. I ordered fish and french fries. Joe ordered a hamburger, as he typically does even at seafood restaurants. And that was the end of the conversation. It was that simple. That's how we've always communicated on the important questions. We get straight to the point. The more it matters, the more efficient we tend to be. And this—possibly the most important conversation of our lives—was less than a minute long. Eventually, we would gather as a family to discuss the election, but big decisions had to be Joe's alone—and this was the biggest decision of all.

I've always let Joe steer his own ship, as he has always let me steer mine. We've always made a point of not second-guessing each other. That doesn't mean we've never disagreed, but we trust each other. Supporting the other's visions—and for a man of his generation, Joe was hugely supportive of my work and my independence—has been one of the great gifts of my marriage and my life.

I was relieved he'd finally decided. Privately, I also felt in my heart that he'd made the right decision. I knew he felt called to serve at the highest possible level. I wanted it for him, and I wanted it for the country. I thought he would make an exceptional president.

Joe officially declared his candidacy on April 25, 2019, via video. I arrived for class at NOVA that day thinking, *My husband just announced that he's running for president of the United States today and here I am teaching writing*. It felt a little surreal.

A few weeks later, I would stand beside him, wearing a jacket with the word LOVE emblazoned on the back, at the Eakins Oval near the Philadelphia Museum of Art as he spoke about the soul of the nation—but from that moment at BlackSalt, I knew that we were in the race. I felt anxious about what it would mean for all of us, but I also felt that we were ready.

CHAPTER 3

One Saturday morning in October 2008, a month before the election that would make Barack Obama president and Joe his VP, I was out on a run through Rockford Park in Wilmington. I had a lot on my mind in addition to the campaign. My mother was very ill, and our son Beau, who served in the Delaware Army National Guard, was preparing for imminent deployment to a combat zone in Iraq. A Secret Service car pulled up beside me.

"We got a call," the agent said. "You have to go home."

I drove straight to Willow Grove. My mother was dying. All my sisters came to the house and got into bed with her. Even though she wasn't conscious, my mother held on until Sunday, when all five of us were there with her, and then she died. As the eldest, I was now the head of the family. We made funeral arrangements. I stayed home for a couple of days and then resumed the campaign.

As soon as my mother's death was announced, Michelle Obama called from the campaign trail. After offering heartfelt condolences, she said, "I'll see you at the funeral." I was overwhelmed by her kindness.

I hadn't gotten to know Michelle when we were both Senate

spouses—I lived in Delaware, she lived in Chicago, and we both had full-time jobs, plus kids in school, so it was rare that we interacted. In spite of our husbands being on the same ticket, and in spite of my admiration of her, we hadn't spent much time together yet, and so I hesitated before I spoke.

"Michelle, I don't know how to tell you this," I said, "but I have four sisters. This funeral is going to be so hard on them, and it has to be about my sisters losing a mother. It can't be just me, right? I'm afraid that if you're there, the press will treat it as a major event and pull focus away from my sisters. Your offer is so incredibly generous, but I think it's better if you don't come. Does that make sense?"

Saying all that felt awkward, but of course Michelle instantly put me at ease.

"I totally get it," she said.

No more had to be said. As someone who'd done her best to cultivate privacy for her own family, she just knew.

I grew up in middle-class America of the 1950s and '60s. I loved my teachers, made my own Christmas gifts, traipsed to the library every week, and rode my bike everywhere. Our parents were often playful with each other. Friends were always stopping by, the house full of people enjoying games like Ping-Pong and checkers.

Our father fought in World War II as a signalman in the Navy, and he was very patriotic. He would take us to watch the Blue Angels, remarking on each awe-inspiring feat of the Navy squadron. He played John Philip Sousa marches on the hi-fi and flew the American flag by our front door on holidays.

If we adored our father, we *worshipped* our mother. We could and did tell her everything—when we went out drinking, our first kisses, who was doing what with whom. She always offered sage advice.

Once, I argued with a friend named Toni over a boy we both liked named Timmy. (Isn't it amazing how names like that stick with us through the years? Until now, I hadn't thought of him since I was a teenager.) Toni called me up and said she wanted to discuss him. My mother said, "You have her come here. You always fight your battles on your own turf." Toni came over to have it out with me, asserting her right to Timmy. In the end, we both decided he wasn't worth it, and he started dating someone else entirely.

My mother had me when she was twenty, so she seemed young to me my whole life. She also had a young spirit. I can barely remember an argument with her. One time, she came after my sisters and me with a hairbrush to punish us for something, but far from being scared of her, we all wound up laughing hysterically—our mother included. She loved to read, and that had a great influence on me, but she was hardly a shrinking violet. She was so vibrant, so passionate, not above starting a food fight. Her death was devastating to my sisters and me.

For me, time with my sisters—who live relatively nearby, in New Jersey and Pennsylvania—is always a great stress reliever, and just *fun*. They love to go to the beach and to cook amazing meals. When we get together, we can say anything to one another. There's such a bond of trust there, a safe space we cherish. During various health crises, my sisters and I have seen one another through the anxiety and the recovery. In times of joy, we are all there to celebrate.

Growing up, the five of us girls were essentially two separate families because of our age differences. My sister Jan's a year behind me, and my sister Bonny is three years behind Jan. The three of us were wrapped up in our parents' unconditional love, with a coziness and routine straight out of *Ozzie and Harriet*.

That said, we had very little money. Jan, Bonny, and I lived through our family's lean years in a small two-bedroom house. For vacations, we might do a day trip to the beach. We never, ever went out to a restaurant. The big treat was packed ice cream on nights when we watched *Ed Sullivan*. The three of us slept in three beds wedged against the walls of one room.

Then, when I was fifteen years old, my mother, at age thirty-five, found herself pregnant—to her surprise, with twins. I was out of the house by the time they were out of diapers, and Kelly and Kim had a totally different childhood. My father's career as a banker had taken off, so the twins grew up in a bigger house, with their own rooms. They stayed at the shore for two weeks on vacation, and they got to buy whatever they wanted—at Lord & Taylor! I'd never been fully aware of the disparity until we started sharing memories as adults. For so many years, I'd been caught in a 1950s time warp, busy with marriage, divorce, a new family, the Senate. How good it has felt to reconnect with my sisters as grown women, some of us now mothers and grandmothers ourselves, with our own achievements and rich lives to share.

We all have roles in a family. As the eldest daughter, I think I've tended to be the strong one, the one who keeps it together when others are unraveling. That's who I've been to my kids, my grandkids, and my sisters, too, particularly since the death of our mother. But with my sisters, I can relax in a way that can be difficult with other people. We know one another so well, and trust one another so fully. They cheered me on as I crisscrossed the country in support of Joe's campaigns. They've kept me grounded, and they value their own privacy as much as they protect mine.

To cope with stress and stay healthy, I've always done my best to work out every day, usually at SoulCycle or Barre3. Once at a Sephora after a cycle class, someone said to Kim, "I just saw Jill Biden!"

"Wow!" Kim said, not mentioning that she was my sister.

I think most women realize the importance of sisterhood—whether it's at work, at church, or at a book club. I've seen how women offer support to one another's families through raising children, coping with illness, and handling financial hardship. I experienced this as a young girl when all the women in my middle-class neighborhood became my "aunts."

In the 1960s and '70s, "sisterhood" became a broader term signifying support for Title IX (the civil-rights-in-education amendment), equal pay for women entering the workforce, and the Equal Rights Amendment. We read *Ms.* magazine and came to see Gloria Steinem as an icon. Still, when Geraldine Ferraro was chosen by Walter Mondale as VP, it was clear that much of the country still found the notion of a woman in that position of power almost unthinkable.

In our middle years, it's the women in our lives who support us through childbirth, or carpooling, or other obligations. Who is the one who leaves a lasagna in your fridge or a roast chicken on your kitchen counter when times are tough?

Jan, Bonny, Kim, Kelly—and my longtime friends Mary Ann and Mary—have done so much to help me through tough times, whether at the White House or in Wilmington. Thanks to my time as First Lady, I have a direct line to practically anyone in the world, and yet when I really need a friend, there's no one I'd rather call than them.

CHAPTER 4

Campaigning is a numbers game, and your luck can change by the minute. In a single car ride, you might have people saluting, people giving you the finger, and people mooning you. Sometimes you make endless calls asking local elected officials to endorse your candidate and to potential donors asking them to support the campaign financially, and great things happen; other times, nothing does. In April 2019, Joe had entered the race, and it was time for both of us to head back out on the trail again. I found that it wasn't difficult for me to speak to crowds about people I cared about and wanted to see in office—the same way I'd been able to find my confidence in front of a classroom.

When Joe first ran for president in the 1988 election, our daughter, Ashley, was in first grade. That summer, I was on the trail constantly, but I made sure to make it home to read to Ashley at bedtime. I was beyond exhausted. But there was so much to do.

During those months, I spent a lot of time traveling to Iowa—sitting in people's homes, talking to them about supporting Joe. I'd be there for hours, telling them about Joe, his positions, and then they'd say, "We need to meet him again—like three more times—to make up our mind." Their indecision was dispiriting. Because Iowa uses a caucus system, voters would have to publicly back you. If you didn't have enough support to be considered viable, your supporters would need to choose another candidate. Some people would say that they'd support you, but then, in the end, they didn't.

When Joe withdrew that September, I heard that a job was opening up at Claymont High School in January, and I took it. A few weeks into that semester, just two days before Valentine's Day, someone from the school's main office knocked on my door to tell me something was very wrong with Joe. I rushed to his side and learned he'd had an aneurysm. I walked into the hospital room just as he was being given last rites. I yelled at the priest to get out—my husband was not going to die.

He had to be taken by ambulance from Saint Francis Hospital in Wilmington to Walter Reed Army Medical Center in Washington, DC—he couldn't be flown because of his medical condition. Instead of the romantic Valentine's weekend we'd planned at an inn in Connecticut, we were on a long, snowy drive between hospitals, his life hanging in the balance. "Way to ruin the holiday," I teased him.

He was out of the Senate recovering for about seven months. He walked back into the chamber in September 1988 to a standing ovation.

Joe next ran for president in 2008. Iowa was once again a challenge. After placing fifth there, Joe dropped out. But before he did, I got a glimpse of where the election was headed. Sitting in the bleachers of the Veterans Memorial Auditorium in Des Moines, I saw how much energy there was behind Barack Obama's candidacy. Obama buses stretched out as far as the eye could see, bringing supporters. Standing near me was an Obama campaign worker in a headset, orchestrating chants. Everywhere I looked, there were round red, white, and blue Obama signs held up by people in I'M FIRED UP T-shirts. As soon as Barack finished his speech, the arena shook with coordinated shouts of "Fired up!" and "Ready to go!" The enthusiasm was palpable.

I couldn't help but think back on those crowds when Joe was running for president again in 2019. The 2020 Democratic primary field was extremely congested: Bernie Sanders, Elizabeth Warren, Tulsi Gabbard, Michael Bloomberg, Amy Klobuchar, Pete Buttigieg, Tom Steyer, Deval Patrick, Michael Bennet, Andrew Yang (surrounded by his "Yang Gang," flocks of young supporters who adored him), Bill de Blasio, Cory Booker, John Delaney, Marianne Williamson, Julián Castro, Kamala Harris, Steve Bullock, Joe Sestak, Beto O'Rourke, Tim Ryan . . . Joe was not the young, sexy candidate—Bernie was!

Primary season began with the Iowa caucuses, followed by a primary in New Hampshire. Iowa has ninety-nine counties, so a candidate has to be extremely organized to do well there. New Hampshire is a test of momentum because it's a ballot race. You have to be able to energize people and get them to come out in the cold.

We spent an enormous amount of time campaigning in those two states. A volunteer named Jodi Grover, an educator from a local college, drove us to nearly all our Iowa campaign events. She logged the distance she and I traveled together to Iowa tour stops from February 2019 to June 2020: 7,447 miles. As we neared each destination, our hype song was "Dance Monkey" by Tones and I. Jodi is a lifelong friend and the best of Iowa. Her mother would often surprise me with her homemade strawberry-rhubarb pie, my favorite.

I arrived at many events in those first two states to find only a handful of people—one time, just two. Still, Joe was led to believe his campaign was still viable. It certainly wasn't my job to second-guess the advisors, so I trusted the process. If Joe wanted to stay in the race, and his team thought he had a shot in spite of what I was seeing on the ground, I would keep showing up.

Candidates tend at one point or another to wind up in a bubble because they're working so hard to raise money and reach voters. I was always trying to get myself out of it, whether by staying in touch with my sisters and friends outside DC or through my job, and I encouraged Joe as much as I could to widen his circle of advisors.

Too often, I'd seen how candidates had been led to believe that their chances were better than they were. I didn't want that to happen to Joe. In March 2019, as the campaign was taking shape, long before the primaries, I'd attended a planning meeting at our home on Chain Bridge Road. Looking around at the advisors, I imagined Joe out on the trail months into the future. I wanted to know how he'd avoid being surprised or disappointed. "Which one of you is going to tell him the truth?" I said, looking around the table.

One advisor said, "I will! I'm going to be the truth-teller!"

Did he? I found myself wondering about that when Joe floundered in the primaries. Joe came in fourth place in Iowa, and fifth in New Hampshire. Especially for a former vice president, the poor showing was remarkable, and Joe was surprised he hadn't done better. I was devastated for him. I couldn't help but suspect that Joe's advisors had been overstating his chance of winning the nomination.

Joe did better in the third primary contest, in Nevada, by which time many of the candidates were running out of money. Joe's campaign chairman, Steve Ricchetti, did some fundraising so Joe had enough to stay in. I would support Joe as long as he stayed in the race, but after New Hampshire, I privately suspected that the campaign was all but over. When the power went out at our hotel on our final night in New Hampshire, it felt like an omen.

Then, on the day of the primary, we flew to Columbia, South Carolina. The enthusiasm for Joe's campaign changed as quickly as the weather. That night, the Bethlehem Baptist Church Mass Choir sang "All in His Hands." Congressman Jim Clyburn would later draw a parallel to how safe our country would be in Joe's care: "I can think of no one better suited, better prepared. I can think of no one with more integrity, no one more committed to the fundamental principles that make this country what it is than my good friend."

That was the turning point. It was actually surreal how abruptly Joe's fortunes shifted. On March 2, the calls started coming in: Beto O'Rourke, Amy Klobuchar, Pete Buttigieg—all were endorsing Joe. That day, I surprised Joe backstage at a rally in Dallas. I could feel the energy in the room; it was the opposite of the sleepy events in chilly New Hampshire. On Super Tuesday, March 3, Joe won ten out of fourteen contests. Endorsements from Michael Bloomberg and Kamala Harris followed on March 4 and 8.

That was a lesson to me in trusting Joe's instincts, and his advisors. Even when a campaign seemed to be over, apparently sometimes you just had to give it a few days and everything could change. On April 8, Bernie Sanders left the race, endorsing Joe, at which point Joe became the presumptive nominee.

In a video posted online, Barack Obama began, "Let me start by saying the obvious: These aren't normal times." He talked about how dire things were, and described the qualities a leader needed to help America make it through the pandemic and to rebuild: "knowledge and experience, honesty and humility, empathy and grace."

"Choosing Joe to be my vice president was one of the best decisions I ever made, and he became a close friend," Barack continued. "And I believe Joe has all the qualities we need in a president right now."

A tough primary was over.

CHAPTER 5

Like so many women I know, I learned to compartmentalize in order to have a full life. It's a survival skill. I am able to go to my exercise class and be fully present there, switch to being in my classroom and entirely a teacher, send valentines to my children and grandchildren, then go to a gala and be Joe's spouse without distraction. I considered it a source of strength. But after Beau's death, holding everything together became much more difficult for me. Finding ways to take care of myself while being present for my family was not easy. Deep grief can be isolating.

Hunter was a successful lawyer, teaching at Georgetown's School of Foreign Service and serving as board chair of World Food Program USA. Beau's death left him unhinged. Joe and I found that our calls to Hunter, then in his mid-forties, often went unanswered. Day after day, the question hung in the air: *Where is he?*

"Have you heard from Hunter?" I would say, putting down my phone.

"No, have you?" Joe would reply.

"No."

"Well, where do you think he is?"

"I don't know."

Addiction was not a topic that Joe and I talked about. I think we were partly in denial. Why would Hunter use drugs? He had everything: a family who loved him, a good education, a lucrative career.

Joe and I tried to manage it as best we could. But then Hunter's daughters came to us asking if we'd help them arrange an intervention. We staged two. The first time, Hunter didn't show up. The second, he arrived to find his family gathered along with a counselor. He turned right around and bolted.

Ultimately, Hunter found the amazing strength to get enduringly sober in 2019. He credits the support of his new wife, Melissa, with keeping him stable and helping him choose the path of sobriety each day.

As a teacher, I had students who would start smoking pot the moment they woke up and were stoned every day in class. I could usually tell when they were high, and I tried to talk to many of them about getting help, about reaching out to counselors. But the answer was always the same: "I don't need help. I can stop on my own. It's okay."

Certainly, when I was teaching English at the Rockford Center psychiatric hospital starting in 1981 while getting my master's degree, I saw serious cases of addiction, and a lot of suffering on the part of both those with addiction and their families. I watched attendants put kids in padded cells for LSD flashbacks. Almost every child in the psychiatric hospital was put there by the courts for attempting suicide. So many young people I encountered took drugs to dull the pain because of abuse in their homes or in foster care. Usually, insurance only allowed a two-week stay. Two weeks. How can you heal a lifetime of trauma in two weeks?

The horror of addiction, for the one suffering and their family, has nevertheless proved a steep learning curve for me. Even now, I can barely say the words "My son was a drug addict." Barely.

The guilt I feel as a parent is sometimes overwhelming. What could I have done differently? What did I do wrong? What did I not see?

Many people have asked why I never took on addiction as a cause as First Lady. I couldn't. I really don't have any answers, even though I deeply empathize with those who love people struggling with addiction. I know the agony of living with the question *Where is my child right now, at this moment?*

The other day, I was cleaning out a drawer and found one of Hunter's lighters, and I was instantly triggered. How many times had I seen him using it, obsessively smoking cigarettes?

Generationally, I was raised to stay stoic and contained. Regardless of how bad it looked, I believed that Hunter would get it together on his own. That's something I regret now, not having tried sooner to talk about it. A lot of people knew how dire the situation had become, but they didn't say anything, and I didn't ask. For years, nothing was spoken aloud about Hunter's addiction—not its effect on him and the family, and not even the grief that had surely compounded the situation. But it's funny how things unsaid sometimes have a way of making themselves heard.

In January 2020, I was on the campaign trail in Concord, New Hampshire. My staff and I made a stop at a Riverbend clinic for a roundtable with mental health professionals.

I talked abstractly, as I generally did, about how it was such an important issue, and how my students had made me aware of mental health challenges. Then a retired doctor there asked me how Joe and I handled mourning our son while also serving the country. I wanted to give him an honest answer, and so I decided I would tell him a bit about what that time had been like.

"Nobody really knew what we were going through," I said. Beau and his family wanted to maintain their privacy, so we'd told no one outside our inner circle about his prognosis. "We had to keep it quiet. So we never received any sort of counseling ourselves or any help for our family to go through that because it was kept so quiet. And Beau, our son, wanted it that way. He didn't want the world to know, and nor did we. It's a very personal thing to go through, as you well know, and a very tough thing to go through."

That's when, perhaps, on any other day I would have stopped. Instead, I heard myself saying something that had been welling up inside me for a long time:

"One of the things that I had to do and Joe had to do . . . I was working at the time. I was teaching, so I would go to the hospital very early in the morning before I taught, or I'd go after I taught, or I'd stay there late into the night. Joe would be in the vice president's office. He'd be working. He'd go there at eleven, twelve, one in the morning and stay all night with Beau. We never left Beau alone."

I remained calm, but I maintained eye contact with that doctor. I felt that he was truly listening, almost asking me follow-up questions without speaking, and so I continued:

"But that, I think, did take a tremendous toll on our family. In the emotional aspect. And the fallout from it. It affected our kids. It affected our grandkids. So we didn't have any support built in. Just because of the nature of the office, actually. And maybe that was a mistake, I don't know. It just wasn't practical. It just wasn't *practical*."

News cameras recorded the conversation, or I wouldn't have believed that I'd said all that. Nobody took particular note of the exchange. For all the tiny gestures the press made so much of, that full-blown confession of how my family had suffered and repressed, repressed and suffered, went entirely unmentioned. For that room full of people whose job it was to bear witness to suffering, it surely wasn't unusual to have someone confess to feeling great pain, nor to second-guess how they'd handled it. But for me, it was unprecedented to share so much.

When we got back in the car, my aide looked at me in shock. "Whoa! What was that about?" he asked.

"I don't know," I said. "I was just looking at all those people working hard to share and get better, and all the people helping them, and I thought, *What would the family be like if we'd had more of that kind of support since Beau died?*"

In May 2019, I was proud to join the opening of a brand-new cancer clinic on Navajo Nation land in Tuba City, Arizona. Patients from the Navajo Nation often had to drive for hours, with no rest areas along the way, to get chemotherapy. The journey was so grueling that many chose to forego care. This new facility would save them from hours of daily round-trip driving to non-Native land for their treatment. It was exactly the sort of improvement in care that I hoped my advocacy work was helping make possible. For as happy an occasion as it was, when I walked into the clinic and saw a chemotherapy chair, it triggered me. I was right back there with Beau, holding his hand. I had to walk down the hallway and pull myself together before I could participate in the opening celebration.

Today, perhaps, politicians can share that they go to therapy. Maybe it would be seen as admirable. But certainly, back in the

1970s and '80s and '90s, it would have been taken as a mark against the family.

Most young people today don't know the name Thomas F. Eagleton, but people my age do. He was a senator, and George McGovern's 1972 Democratic vice presidential candidate for eighteen days before he was forced out because it was revealed that he'd battled depression and had electroshock therapy. A few years after that, Joe and I had dinner with Tom and his wife, Barbara. The first time I stepped into their home, she took one look at my super-high, strappy heels with a bow on the front and said, "I see you're wearing your 'f**k-me' shoes."

I burst out laughing. *Nobody* talked like that back then, not in the circles we ran in. I decided two things in that moment: One, I wanted to be Barbara's friend. She was hilarious and I loved her. Two, I should get a second pair of those shoes.

For the most part, I've been able to hold myself together, moving forward without letting anyone see when I'm in pain. Not everyone is built that way. Some people are just more sensitive. If they're sad, they cry in public. When they hit a rough patch, you can see the wheels come off. I used to think my way was the healthier path. Now I'm not so sure.

CHAPTER 6

Joe's presidential campaign enjoyed the post–Super Tuesday momentum for a little over a week before the campaign was grounded by COVID. Across America, people began finding ways to stay connected and to work from a distance. A stay-at-home order was issued in Delaware on March 22, and the campaign pivoted to doing virtual events.

We built one cold little studio on the back patio and another in the basement so Joe and I could both do back-to-back Zooms all day. To bring people together and get Joe's message out, the campaign got creative. At car rallies, fashioned after drive-in movie theaters, the enthusiasm came through: "Honk if you want America to be united again!" We held these rallies all over Pennsylvania, Michigan, Florida, and Ohio. One Toledo event with autoworkers was held outside a union hall.

For one fundraiser, Food Network superstar Ina Garten conducted an online cocktail-making class called "Cocktails and Conversation." She and I chatted and created a cocktail-hour energy for donors. The set was decorated with watermelons carved with messages like BIDEN 2020. We'd sent a list of ingredients out before the event so everyone could enjoy the same signature drink: the Winning Ticket

Watermelon Cosmopolitan. We had so much fun. I loved Ina's energy and humor.

She'd gone viral in April for the Quarantine Cosmo, which I think kept a large part of the country tipsy throughout the spring. She started with two cups of vodka and one cup of Cointreau. "You need a big pitcher . . . You never know who's stopping by," she said. "Wait a minute—nobody's stopping by!"

As it became safer to travel, we put exacting COVID protocols in place. The campaign paid to test us all daily. Our temperature was taken before we got onto the plane—a biometric boarding pass. We wore masks and gloves to keep ourselves safe and to set an example.

While I spent time talking to voters about Joe, we often joined local pandemic aid efforts. I will never forget the depth of the wounds. Many middle-class families had to turn to food banks. As we loaded their cars, drivers told me that they had never asked for help before, but they'd been pushed to the brink.

People were struggling in so many ways. They were afraid of getting sick, wondering how they were going to afford food, and they were scared for their kids. Nurses and doctors were overwhelmed by the overcrowding at hospitals and were unable to get the personal protective equipment they needed.

The economy had been devastated. One woman came up to me on the campaign trail and said that her husband, a farmer, had seen his livelihood destroyed by tariffs. "The first time we had trouble, he was okay," she said. "The second time, he just couldn't endure it. He killed himself. I'm left with the farm, and I'm not sure what I'm going to do."

People kept saying they were sick of holding their breath, wondering what outrageous thing the president would do next. They wanted to be able to breathe again.

Throughout the 2020 campaign, Joe promised that, if elected, his administration and cabinet would "look like the country." He committed to putting a Black woman on the Supreme Court and to picking a woman as his running mate. I was proud of Joe. It was time. He would do what no Democrat had done since Walter Mondale asked Geraldine Ferraro to be on his ticket back in 1984.

Once Joe was the official nominee, the campaign staff began generating names to consider as his potential running mate. Candidates on their first list included Minnesota Senator Amy Klobuchar, Florida Congresswoman Val Demings, California Congresswoman Karen Bass, Michigan Governor Gretchen Whitmer, California Senator Kamala Harris, Rhode Island Governor Gina Raimondo, Massachusetts Senator Elizabeth Warren, Illinois Senator Tammy Duckworth, former Georgia House Minority Leader Stacey Abrams, and Obama's national security advisor, Susan Rice. They were all vetted.

Joe asked me to sit in on the candidate meetings so that he could ask for my impressions later. Most of the meetings with the candidates were on Zoom, but we were able to arrange a couple of in-person visits. Gretchen Whitmer came to Rehoboth Beach, Delaware. She flew in secretly by jet with her state's lead police officer, and we interviewed her at the house. I liked her story. I liked her grit. I liked her strength.

Former police chief and Florida Congresswoman Val Demings, I loved. She's from Jacksonville. In March, I had a great day on the primary trail with Val and her husband, Jerry, mayor of Orange County and the former county sheriff. They have three children and five grandchildren, and she rides motorcycles. She took me with one of her granddaughters to a church service with a DJ and rock music. The service was broadcast all over the state, and thousands of people tuned in. I found the energy in that place of worship particularly refreshing, because I was raised Presbyterian. We sat in the pews and nobody said a word. You didn't look around. You just sat there and thought to yourself about who in your row was singing the loudest—it was always my grandmother.

I first heard Kamala Harris's name around 2011. One Sunday dinner, Beau told us about her: "Mom, I met someone to watch! Her name is Kamala Harris." They were both attorneys general, working together on the post–financial crisis multistate mortgage fraud and foreclosure settlement. He had high praise for her. Joe and I took note the way you do when your kids tell you about something that impresses them. She went on to be elected senator of California and began to look at a presidential run.

Then, in the June 2019 debate, Kamala had turned to Joe and criticized him for how he'd voted on busing as a way to desegregate schools. Her sharp conclusion: "There was a little girl in California who was part of the second class to integrate her public schools, and she was bused to school every day. That little girl was me."

The thought bubble above my head was full of expletives, but sitting in the crowd that night, I knew I couldn't let anyone see me react.

I could see Joe was caught off guard, surprised to be hit with what amounted to a "gotcha" moment.

"I did not oppose busing in America," Joe said. "What I opposed is busing ordered by the Department of Education. That's what I opposed . . . I ran because of civil rights . . . I'm the guy that extended the voting rights for twenty-five years."

But of course the clip that ran the day after the debate was Kamala turning to Joe and implying that his busing policy—a stance not all that different from her own—made him a racist. To me, it seemed like hypocritical point-scoring.

Joe had long enjoyed strong support from Black voters, particularly older Black voters, because he'd fought alongside them for decades even against stiff opposition. As a senator, he'd pushed to get federal investment into Black neighborhoods and to unify areas that had been torn apart by highways put there by eminent domain. As president, Joe would keep his promise to promote diversity on federal benches, appointing sixty-three Black judges, including forty women, to lifetime appointments, and to put the first Black woman on the Supreme Court. He would make Juneteenth a national holiday and sign the Emmett Till Antilynching Act.

In politics, you learn to let things go. Joe quickly moved on, and Kamala dropped out of the race in early December 2019.

Joe invited her to the Chain Bridge Road house for a meeting in person on July 27 to discuss the possibility of her becoming his running mate. She was warm and chatted easily with the staff about how she'd just made enchiladas with her husband, Doug Emhoff.

Right off the bat, Joe told Kamala she was one of the top choices. She responded instantly by making a strong case for herself. She mentioned the personal connection she felt to our family, and spoke about how much she'd cared about Beau. After about half an hour, the meeting wrapped up. Joe and I agreed that we were impressed by her. She was definitely in the running.

As pressure grew to announce Joe's choice for VP—it's customary to do this a couple of weeks before the convention—he said, "Let's do this: You put your top three down on a piece of paper and I'll put my top three, and we'll seal them in separate envelopes." We did this four times—once a week, we would write down our choices, open the envelopes, and read the names. The first three lists were completely different. We never opened the last pair of envelopes.

Then it was time for him to make his choice. The envelope exercise was fun, but at the end of the day, I was Joe's spouse. Of course he had to make the call on his own.

It had been a hard decision for Joe; the candidates all had their own set of strengths. But judging by the polls, and informed by the eight years he'd spent in the role himself, the choice was clear: Kamala Harris.

The video that introduced me at the 2020 Democratic National Convention—which had to take place mostly online—opened with the story of how Joe and I met.

"When I met Jill, I knew," Joe recalled. "My brother said, 'There's this woman. You'd really like her, Joe,' so I gave her a call and she had a date that night." He said he'd asked me to break that date to go out with him instead. "And what'd you do?" He turned to me.

I said I'd called and told the other guy that I had a friend who'd come to town. I went out with Joe instead.

I loved that Joe was from a slightly earlier era than I was. Dating after I divorced my first husband, I found some of the men I went out with took women's liberation and free love as a sign that I was theirs to grope. Unlike them, Joe respected me. He was gallant, and I looked up to him. After our first date, he shook my hand goodnight. I ran upstairs and called my mother at one o'clock in the morning. "Mom," I said, "I finally met a gentleman."

He's still that man. To this day, he calls me "his girl." People who sit next to him at dinner have been known to come up to me afterward to say, "He loves you *so much*." To which I say, "He talked your ear off, didn't he?"

Joe was a thirty-year-old widower raising two boys, so our dates weren't the usual courtship. It was always the four of us going to the movies, to the beach, to dinner. Joe said he was shaving one morning when the boys ran in before school and said, "Dad, we think it's time to marry Jill." Joe proposed five times. The children had already been through so much. I knew if I said yes, it would have to be forever, so I waited until I was absolutely sure. On the fifth proposal, I said yes. The truth is that I loved him from the start.

Knowing that we wouldn't be gathering in a large forum because of COVID, I chose to give my convention speech from my classroom at Brandywine High School in Wilmington, where I'd taught in the early 1990s. In a green dress, I walked down the hallway and said, "I have always loved the sounds of a classroom. The quiet that sparks with possibility just before students shuffle in, the murmur of ideas bouncing back and forth as we explore the world together, the laughter and tiny moments of surprise you find in materials you've taught a million times."

The empty, silent school—with no scent of new notebooks or freshly waxed floors—to me conveyed the huge cost of the pandemic. What would get us to the other side of the crisis was taking care of one another.

"I never imagined at the age of twenty-six I would be asking myself, 'How do you make a broken family whole?'" I said from that echoey school. "Still, Joe always told the boys, 'Mommy sent Jill to us.' And how could I argue with her? And so we figured it out together . . . We found that love holds a family together. Love makes us flexible and resilient. It allows us to become more than ourselves, together, and though it can't protect us from the sorrows of life, it gives us refuge, a home. How do you make a broken family whole? The same way you make a nation whole: With love and understanding and with small acts of kindness. With bravery, with unwavering faith. We show up for each other in big ways and small ones again and again . . .

"We just need leadership worthy of our nation. Worthy of you. Honest leadership to bring us back together, to recover from this pandemic and prepare for whatever else is next. Leadership to reimagine what our nation will be. That's Joe. He and Kamala will work as hard as you do every day to make this nation better. And if I have the honor of serving as your First Lady, I will, too. And with Joe as president, these classrooms will ring out with laughter and possibility once again."

In the weeks leading up to the election, when we held gatherings in person, we set out Hula-Hoops on the ground to help maintain distance. I'd look out on the crowd of masked people, each one standing in their own Hula-Hoop, and think about how we were living in strange times. I was also just so happy to be away from the computer screen. In the presence of other people, I could feel the energy and support behind Joe. I didn't want to take anything for granted, but I believed that he would win.

The results weren't final as states recounted, so Election Day became Election Week. Held in suspense, we were hopeful, but wouldn't allow ourselves to feel overly confident. In Wilmington, I had a houseful of family—our kids and grandkids had been with us for days. On Thursday, we turned up the music and started a kitchen dance party to relieve some tension. Yet in the background was the ever-present Steve Kornacki in those tan slacks, standing before that whiteboard. Had he changed clothes? Had he showered? Had he slept? Was he human?

Late on Saturday morning, Joe and I decided we had to get away from the TVs, so we filled up our coffee cups and went down to sit on the dock by the lake. We heard a roar coming from the house. The grandkids came running down the lawn screaming, "We won! We won!"

Joe had won. Decisively in both the popular vote and the Electoral College, and with historically high turnout from a broad coalition. After so much instability, Joe would help the country finally get back to normal. Nothing that election year had been normal. The primary wasn't normal because there were almost thirty Democratic candidates. The campaign wasn't normal because of COVID. The win wasn't normal because there was no concession. Nothing followed the normal pattern. So we should not have been surprised that the inauguration wouldn't be normal either.

CHAPTER 7

On January 6, we were at home in Wilmington packing up to move into the White House. The day before, I'd filled the last available position on my team and was feeling good about the staff I'd hired. Joe was working on an economic speech he was scheduled to deliver that afternoon. When we heard that there was some kind of attack underway at the Capitol, we turned on the TV and couldn't believe what we were seeing. Rioters smashing windows, running around the building, yelling and grabbing papers off of desks? How could this be happening?

In every image we saw, we scanned the crowd. I caught a glimpse of Delaware Representative Lisa Blunt Rochester crouching behind some chairs. We learned that at least one person had been shot. I prayed for the police officers, guards, and staff, so many of whom we knew well.

To Joe, the Senate was practically a holy site. He had so much respect for the institution's history and its protocols. I saw the horror and pain on his face as he watched the footage of rioters trashing the place, threatening the lives of his colleagues.

As the protesters ransacked the Capitol building, the president tweeted that Mike Pence "didn't have the courage" necessary for what had to be done, which was to block or reject the certified electoral votes. This amounted to rejecting America's legal election of Joe. In the building, rioters began hunting for Vice President Pence, calling him a traitor. A chant went up: "Hang Mike Pence!" Outside on the lawn, gallows were erected. This was unbelievable.

We got on the phone to friends and staff members in DC to see if they were okay and if there was anything we could do. We begged them to stay alert and to be careful. I was terrified for them, and for the country. Was this a coup, the end of democracy? Was it possible Joe's election wouldn't be certified, and even though he'd won the election, he wouldn't become president? All day, we watched the television, stunned.

Finally, the Capitol Police received reinforcements from the DC police, the FBI, and eventually the National Guard. By the time the sun set, order was restored. Even after the city came under control, though, so many of us remained on edge—shocked by the day's violence.

Vice President Pence, despite very real threats to his own life, chose to remain at the Capitol rather than fleeing so that once it was safe, he could do his constitutional duty and oversee the congressional certification. He and so many brave officers, aides, military members, and politicians on both sides of the aisle thought fast and behaved with phenomenal courage. They protected our shared democracy, and they saved lives.

As the National Guard established wider perimeters around landmarks and the mayor enacted a curfew, Washington felt safer but remained shaken. Joe was to be inaugurated just two weeks later, on January 20. Creating a festive atmosphere was hard under the circumstances. Many of the people we invited to perform were scared of getting COVID or of being attacked by a mob.

At the height of a divisive pandemic, after an insurrection, Joe wanted his inauguration to be focused on unity and joy, and it was.

One beacon of joy was the young poet Amanda Gorman, whom I was glad to have chosen. During the planning phase, Joe had been sitting in the sunroom talking on the phone to his friend Secretary John Kerry, and John had made a recommendation for a poet to read at the inauguration. Joe had so many decisions to make. He said, "Okay, I'll consider it."

When he got off the phone, he turned to me and said, "You know poetry. Help me with this one."

I went online to check out John's recommendation. His poet had a Harvard affiliation and seemed to be a good choice. But in going down the rabbit hole online after finding that person, I somehow wound up watching a young poet speak at the inauguration of Harvard's president in 2018. She was electrifying.

I reached out to Amanda to see if she'd be willing to read at Joe's inauguration, and she was. Then she almost canceled on us because she had security concerns due to the insurrection. Everyone was nervous. We had to persuade her, as well as Lady Gaga and Jennifer Lopez, that it would be safe enough for them to be there. We believed there were enough protocols in place to ensure everyone's safety, but we also didn't know what surprises there might be.

Before I left for Washington on January 19, I taught my class over Zoom from Wilmington. The second semester at Northern Virginia Community College was beginning the week of the inauguration.

I'd always loved the first day of school, and even in this modified format, I looked forward to getting to know a new batch of students. I always wondered: What had brought them to college? What did they want to do? How could I help them do it?

Every class had a different dynamic. I might have a group that was predominantly made up of quick-witted young men, and we'd joke our way through the class period. Another might be mostly women returning to school following years of caregiving, and I'd notice how voraciously they read, how delighted they seemed to be doing something for themselves.

When COVID separated us physically, we had to find new ways to reach students who needed mentoring and guidance. I was moved to see that students still got themselves to show up every day, in spite of all that they were dealing with. Now, with many of their own children at home and attending school virtually, those hardships were compounded. I noticed that semester's students trying to carve out spaces in their homes to attend class online, even with children hanging on their shoulders or scooting behind them. When I asked one student to turn on his camera, he said he couldn't because his guinea pig had chewed through the wire. *Good story*, I thought, and let it go.

In that first class, I went over the syllabus and gave them their first journal assignment. I told them they'd have to do a research paper but encouraged them not to be intimidated by its length. We'd take it one paragraph at a time, I said. It would be okay, even fun. I wanted to ease any anxiety they had about writing so they felt that it was within their ability.

From there, I headed to the airport, to begin the inauguration festivities.

Joe and I arrived at Joint Base Andrews at dusk and were driven straight to the Lincoln Memorial. On the way in, I stared incredulously at the way the city had been transformed by the events of January 6, not two weeks earlier. The National Guard stood sentinel. We saw tanks set up on street corners. Non-scalable fencing had been erected everywhere. There were extra layers of security at every turn. The streets had already been emptier than usual because of COVID, but they seemed even bleaker now.

Once we arrived, I walked arm in arm with Joe toward the Reflecting Pool. I'd chosen to wear a purple coat, the color of unity, with butterflies on the lining as a symbol of hope. Next to us, by the water, stood Vice President–Elect Kamala Harris and Doug Emhoff. Off to the side at a respectful distance stood aides and the Secret Service. Everyone was masked. The mood was solemn as night began to fall, and the air grew colder.

Standing at a lectern, Cardinal Wilton D. Gregory, archbishop of Washington, and the first-ever Black Catholic cardinal, took off his mask and began his invocation: "At this twilight hour, our beloved nation reverently pauses in supplication to remember and to pray for the many thousands of people who have died from the coronavirus during this past year." He talked about finding comfort in the memory of our lost loved ones.

Kamala described the pain of losing a loved one who was your whole world, and about how in coming together, we could comfort one another. Lori Marie Key, a nurse who'd become famous online for singing during a shift change at the COVID-19 unit of her Michigan hospital, belted out "Amazing Grace."

Then Joe spoke. He praised nurses, and then said, "To heal, we must remember." Behind him, four hundred lights illuminated the water, honoring the four hundred thousand who had died of

COVID in the United States. As we stood and gazed out at the lights on the water, remembering those we'd lost, the gospel singer Yolanda Adams brought us home with "Hallelujah."

After the ceremony, we drove to Blair House, the official White House guest residence where foreign dignitaries typically stay. Made up of four connected townhouses on Pennsylvania Avenue and facing Lafayette Park, Blair House is breathtaking, with more than 120 rooms, including fourteen guest rooms, each with full bathrooms. Because it's reserved for diplomatic use, I'd never spent time there before and was as dazzled as everyone else.

While thawing out from our time in the cold, we had a rehearsal for the swearing-in ceremony, and then we were told that Jimmy and Rosalynn Carter were on the phone. Joe and I took the call in the sitting room outside our bedroom. As they congratulated Joe, the Carters sounded elated. That call meant a lot to us, and it made the whole thing feel more real.

With that, we were released to our family. When we walked into the Lee Dining Room, with its lush blue-and-white window treatments, crystal chandelier, and gilt mirror (we were told this was the *informal* dining room), we were surrounded by people we loved. We hugged the kids and grandkids who'd gathered for Joe's last night as president-elect. Everyone seemed giddy, from Joe to Hunter's son, Baby Beau, who was just ten months old.

As I scanned the assembled group—Hunter and his daughters Naomi, Finnegan, and Maisy; Naomi's future husband, Peter; Melissa; Baby Beau; Ashley; and Beau's children, Natalie and Hunter—all talking a mile a minute, eating pasta, and smiling, I said a prayer of gratitude for how happy everyone looked that night.

As soon as we'd finished eating, we went exploring. None of us could get over the beauty of the Blair House. We wandered from room to room admiring every detail. The Jackson Place Sitting Room had a gorgeous mural of white clouds and green trees arrayed around DC landmarks. The library had more than a thousand books of US history, as well as displayed gifts from foreign delegations. We gazed at a particularly gorgeous pale green wallpaper with a floral and avian motif—Was that a robin? Were those carnations? At last, we all admitted we were exhausted. Many of us had to be up before dawn for hair and makeup, so we all went to bed early and sank into our fluffy beds.

Early the next morning, the women gathered in Blair House's salon. We sat drinking coffee in our bathrobes as the blow-dryers whirred. In another room, Joe was going over his speech one more time.

Once everyone was ready, we went to the Cathedral of St. Matthew the Apostle for inaugural Mass. That's where we joined friends and other members of the family. Throughout the church, I spotted members of both political parties, including Nancy Pelosi, Mitch McConnell, Chuck Schumer, and Kevin McCarthy.

The Mass began promptly, and it was a solemn one. Father Kevin O'Brien, whom Joe and I had known for fifteen years, preached on our duty to take care of those in need. "We have much to look forward to as a country because of your and Kamala Harris's leadership," he said to Joe. "Every day, you will strive to heal our nation's wounds and reconcile differences and bring us together. You know too well the challenges ahead and the cost of service."

The opera singer Renée Fleming sang "America the Beautiful" and "Ave Maria." A young singer from the cathedral choir sang Joe's favorite hymn, "On Eagle's Wings."

The traditional tea at the White House for the incoming and outgoing presidents was not being offered, so we went right from the church service to the Capitol.

As the time of the inauguration approached, my emotions built. Everything was timed down to the minute. The climactic moment came for Joe and me to stand behind the double doors of the west side of the Capitol building. Through the wood, we heard the triumphant sound of the military honor fanfare, four ruffles and flourishes; then, "Ladies and gentlemen, the president-elect of the United States, Joseph Robinette Biden Jr., and Dr. Jill Biden."

I could feel a swelling within my chest, like how it feels right before you start to cry. I caught myself before the tears came and stayed calm. The doors opened; the light hit our faces. Smiling behind our masks, we proceeded to our seats.

The skies were gray and there were flurries of snow, but as the inauguration unfolded, the sun began to shine. Senator Amy Klobuchar, chair of the inauguration committee, spoke in her introductory remarks about light breaking through into the darkness and warmth coming in the coldest moments.

In a bright yellow coat and red headband, Amanda Gorman delivered a moving tribute to democracy, "The Hill We Climb." I was thrilled by what she did, and relieved that it had worked out. Her face was radiant, so full of life and energy, and her poem was moving but also accessible. I loved how young she was, only twenty-two, and yet so confidently commanding the crowd.

Lady Gaga was phenomenal in her Schiaparelli ensemble, including a poufy red silk skirt and a massive dove-of-peace brooch. Joe and Gaga had built a relationship years before when she asked him, as the author of the 1994 Violence Against Women Act, to introduce her at the 2016 Academy Awards when she performed "Til It Happens to You." She sang the national anthem. Then J.Lo performed "This Land Is Your Land"—another stunning performance. We had known her since the vice presidency, and she'd endorsed Joe in October 2020. Finally, Garth Brooks sang "Amazing Grace," then hugged the Bushes, Obamas, and Clintons with enthusiasm. When he accepted the invitation, he said that he'd wanted to sing there even though he'd been a lifelong Republican, as a statement of unity.

We felt so much pride when Kamala was sworn in, with Doug standing by her side as their family looked on. Joe had kept his promise and given the country its first woman vice president. Mike and Karen Pence stood by respectfully watching her take the oath. Carrying forth traditions keeps a country stable and whole.

Then it was time for Joe's swearing in. Just eight years earlier, I'd been standing where Doug was, and now there I was, where Michelle Obama had been. It seemed at once like a dream and also so natural. A lifetime coming. It came later in his life than Joe had hoped, but maybe this was always meant to be the time he was called to serve—when the country needed wisdom, calm, experience, humility. It was a time of national grief, and this was a man who'd known more than his share of grief.

"The world breaks everyone and afterward many are strong at the broken places," wrote Ernest Hemingway. I believed that was true of Joe. For all he'd been through, he was stronger. His pain made him empathetic, and his empathy made him better able to lead.

Watching him take the oath of office, I believed with all my heart that Joe had a pivotal part to play in America's history. He had the character, fortitude, and empathy to move the country forward. There was so much fear out there—of threats to democracy, of the virus, of the chaos. Joe could fix it, if anyone could.

As the ceremony ended, Joe, Ashley, Hunter, and I hugged. *If only Beau had lived to see this*, I knew we were all thinking. I heard myself say it out loud: "Beau is here with us." We pulled each other closer.

As we walked up the front steps of the White House, I felt the weight of history on us. The mahogany doors closed behind us, and the president's military band began to play. We passed through the enormous Roman columns and stepped over the marble threshold. Turning around, I saw the crystal chandelier reflecting off the marble floor, and the grandeur of the front hall made me catch my breath. The presidential seal above the Blue Room served as a powerful reminder of the journey ahead, and the legacy of those who had come before.

We resolved to create a new beginning for the country after four years of toxic politics, now compounded by pandemic anxiety. Because of COVID, we couldn't do the usual balls and parties. This was the first inauguration held during a pandemic in a hundred years, and the feeling of isolation was felt by everyone. There was no real celebration of what we'd all achieved together. We were unable to host our supporters as we had at the end of every other campaign. We could not even shake the hands of the people who'd helped get Joe elected, much less host them in Washington for a gala to show our gratitude.

To mark the moment, the inaugural committee created a TV special called *Celebrating America*. Tom Hanks hosted, and we showcased heroes and musicians all over America. Bruce Springsteen sang "Land of Hopes and Dreams" at the Lincoln Memorial. Jon Bon Jovi sang "Here Comes the Sun" on a Miami boardwalk under a cloudy sky at daybreak. The night and the special ended with Joe, me, Kamala, and

Doug watching as fireworks were launched over the National Mall and Katy Perry sang "Firework."

Those songs' lyrics all spoke to the spirit of that day: We'd leave our sorrows behind. Faith would be rewarded. The vaccine would be distributed nationwide. Schools would safely reopen. Joe's rescue plan would go into practice. Poverty rates would plummet. There would be more jobs. The country would remember how good unity felt and how much we could do if we stuck together. The sun would come out.

That first night in the White House, Joe stayed up late walking the grandkids from room to room, exploring. Ashley joined me in front of the fireplace, where I had a glass of wine and tried to take it all in.

Following an inspirational prayer service at the National Cathedral via Zoom the morning after the inauguration, my team got right to work. We'd scheduled online calls with teachers to thank them for all their help and to make sure they knew that this White House would support them as the schools continued to navigate reopening—and ideally not with students inside their own little individual plexiglass boxes, as was the case in some schools early on.

On that first day, I sent the National Guard a video thanking them. Because Beau had served in that branch of the military for a dozen years, I knew how hard they worked even in more peaceful times. Since the insurrection, they'd been enduring countless hardships. I made sure to go and hand out baskets of chocolate chip cookies to troops stationed nearby as a token of appreciation for helping keep the city safe during the inauguration, and to acknowledge how much they'd been through.

Wayne Gretzky, the famous hockey player (I'm a Philadelphia Flyers fan), once said, "You miss 100 percent of the shots you don't take." After eight years as Second Lady, I was prepared to get to work right away. I felt like I knew the role, and I hit the ground running.

I'd taught English in public high school for thirteen years, so I knew how crucial it was that the person "at the top" understood the challenges of classroom teachers and school employees. When I came home from work, I was truly exhausted after not only teaching five classes a day but also filling in for cafeteria duty and study hall, fielding calls from parents asking me to help their children with their college applications, and breaking up fights between students. How many times had we been asked to spend time at meetings or fulfill other obligations that just weren't possible with several classes of thirty-five students each? Where did they think we'd find extra time?

Joe had made a campaign promise that he would appoint a secretary of education who had been a teacher in the public school system. I was thrilled when he nominated Miguel Cardona, who'd started out as a fourth-grade teacher and become the youngest principal in Connecticut. Teachers seemed excited about the appointment—one of their own would have a seat at the table.

When Joe was VP, Michelle Obama and I had worked with military families through the initiative Joining Forces, and I wanted to get the project back up and running right away. I knew how important it was, for example, to ensure that kids with special needs could transfer their individual educational programs (IEPs) from one state to the next rather than go through testing every single time the family was redeployed.

As First Lady, I sought to make it easier for military spouses to work. They wanted to continue with their careers—not to mention it's tough to raise a family on a single income. Spending so much time with military families, I saw how difficult it was for service members' spouses to carve out their own lives when their partners' jobs required them to pick up and move so often. They lived with so much uncertainty around the timing of deployments.

We often talked about ways they could nurture their own interests and if there might be work they could do that had meaning for them. Along with various chambers of commerce, I encouraged companies to step up and increase the number of military spouse hires as part of the Hiring Our Heroes initiative. Several big companies did just that.

In small and large ways, we hoped to make a real difference. People's lives would get better. The task seemed impossible, but I felt like Joe could do so much to help the country—by supporting researchers and doctors in fighting COVID, by trying to lower prices, and by leading with humility and compassion. That's something I worry people may have forgotten in all that came after.

CHAPTER 8

"On Wednesday, you will sit down for a thirty-minute joint interview with the president for the cover of *People* magazine. You will be interviewed on camera by *People*'s national political correspondent . . ."

The memo prepping me for an interview the week after the inauguration was thorough and thoughtful, as always. The communications team provided these to ensure that I knew what to expect and had thought through my answers to likely questions. Our goal in this appearance would be to showcase our first week in the White House.

In a meeting, our teams went over the memo's questions: "What was going through your mind on Inauguration Day?" "How did you spend your first night in the White House, and how did it feel?" "What drew you to the designers and dresses you chose to wear on Inauguration Day?"

We talked through the answers I'd give. Then the communications team flagged this potential question: "You're making history by keeping your teaching job at Northern Virginia Community College. Why did you decide to continue teaching?"

"Before you answer that," someone said, "are you sure you *want* to keep teaching?"

I'd started teaching English that semester via Zoom on the day before the inauguration. Did they really expect me to drop the class now? I didn't say anything. So I was asked again, as if they thought perhaps I just hadn't heard the question the first time.

"If they push you to answer if you're going to keep teaching, what will you say?"

"I'll say yes, I'll do it."

"Why would you need that?" came the reply.

"Why would I need to keep doing what I love to do?" I said. "Are you really asking me that? Because every day is an adventure. Because I feel inspired to go to work. Because it's my calling."

"Well, you're not going to continue to draw a salary, are you?"

"What do you mean?" I said, trying to stay calm. "I've been working there for a long time. I'm paid the same thing everyone else is who does what I do who's been there that long. You want me to quit, or keep doing the job but give the money back?"

Evidently, they did.

They underestimated how hard I'd fought for my own career, how much it meant to women of my generation to have accomplished that. "Make your own money" is one of the key pieces of advice I give girls and women. "You need to know that if something happens, you can take care of yourself."

When women came and asked me for work advice, I told them the workplace today seems far more willing to respect difference, tolerate honesty, and look beyond the Ivy League degree and the flashy résumé. Given my background, I've always had a soft spot for a nontraditional path. I'm more impressed by those who overcome adversity than by those who believe they're owed something because they played the game right.

When my first marriage ended in my mid-twenties, I was thrown into a financial panic. I'd married at eighteen. I didn't have a career or even a college degree. My then-husband owned a popular college bar that he held on to. I wound up with less than a quarter of what I imagined to be our shared money. I swore that I would never be in that vulnerable position again. I couldn't very well preach independence for my whole life and then throw it out the window the second I was living in a fancy house because of my husband's position, could I?

Yet that's what seemed to be expected of me. Didn't I recall how much people had criticized Hillary Clinton for trying to take a policy role in her husband's administration and how no First Lady had ever held a paying job outside of the White House during her husband's time in office? They suggested that I was underestimating how hard it would be to throw state dinners, but, hey, maybe volunteering could be an option! Had I thought about volunteering? Eleanor Roosevelt volunteered! Why didn't I look to Eleanor Roosevelt as a role model? At first, even Joe wasn't sure I could pull off a full teaching schedule given my responsibilities as First Lady.

Usually I sought compromise. But this was not one of those times. Teaching was nonnegotiable for me. Once they were done making their case, I said, "Listen, I'm going to keep teaching at NOVA, so I'm afraid you'll just have to figure it out."

Eventually my working outside of the White House came to be seen as a badge of honor for the administration. The official word became that everyone supported the idea all along.

The dual roles did require some orchestration. Many times, I would change into a First Lady outfit in the school bathroom or in a car on the way to an event. Or after teaching, I would take a twenty-minute cat nap and then get up, do hair and makeup, get dressed, and head out to fulfill my duties as a hostess or guest.

During the pandemic, I taught online from my East Wing office. I'd go in early before anyone else was there, and I'd set up for my lesson. Over Zoom, I would teach the students how to write an essay, help them brush up on grammar, or lead a discussion on a piece of literature. Typically, we'd finish around three, at which point I'd assign homework, upload it into Canvas (a learning management system used by schools), and then shut down my computer for the day.

My job made me a better First Lady. Being on campus grounded me, and helped me stay in touch with what real people were dealing with in a way that can be hard if you're in a White House bubble. Every day, I saw the struggles of my students and what they were going through. For many of them, when campus reopened in August 2021, it was more than ever not just where they received an education—it was a lifeline. One student came to class a week after his father had died by suicide. His classmates and I rallied around him, glad he'd trusted us enough to show up rather than drop out and be consumed by the grief alone. I shared with them literature that had helped me through difficult times in my own life, and encouraged them to see poetry as a refuge.

While I permitted conversation about all sorts of difficult topics, I kept politics outside of the classroom.

If they said, "Dr. B., can I ask you a question?" I said, "If it has anything to do with politics, no."

They couldn't have their phones out in class, but I always knew when they were sneaking a look, because their faces would glaze over. One day, I noticed that look on a student's face, and I went to his desk and reached for the phone. He brought it out from under his desk and put it in my hand.

"I was just googling," he said.

"What are you googling?"

I looked down at the phone. He was googling me. We both cracked up. It was hard to blend in as I walked to the library or the women's center trailed by Secret Service agents, but many students remained oblivious to my life outside the classroom.

I liked it that way. I was happy to be Dr. B. for a few hours a week, to be able to do what I did best, to see a clear difference in the students' work from one paper to the next as things that were hard for them got a little easier.

That's why the *Wall Street Journal* op-ed that landed a month after Joe won felt like such a bizarre attack. It was sent to me by my staff at six in the morning as part of the round-up of news: a hit piece by Joseph Epstein with the headline "Is There a Doctor in the White House? Not if You Need an M.D."

The article began: "Madame First Lady—Mrs. Biden—Jill—kiddo: a bit of advice on what may seem like a small but I think is a not unimportant matter. Any chance you might drop the 'Dr.' before your name? 'Dr. Jill Biden' sounds and feels fraudulent, not to say a touch comic."

I received my doctorate from the University of Delaware at age fifty-five. It took me fifteen years to get that degree, plus two master's (one from West Chester University in 1981 and one from Villanova in 1987), because while raising three kids and teaching full-time, I was only able to take a course a semester. Going back to school was one of the most meaningful personal decisions of my life, and among the toughest. I did it for myself. I earned the degree and was happy that my students would be calling me "Dr. B." from then on.

It felt strange to be attacked for using an honorific that I'd earned. I did wonder if he'd address a man with the condescension with which he chastised me. Somehow I couldn't see him calling Dr. Woodrow Wilson "kiddo."

I was buoyed by the support of Michelle Obama and Bernice King, who tagged me online and said, "My father was a non-medical doctor. And his work benefited humanity greatly. Yours does, too."

My mother was very happy as a homemaker, but I knew that role wasn't for me. The summer I turned sixteen, I got a job. I wanted my own money. I wanted to be able to buy my own things. I went down and worked at the Jersey Shore the whole summer between eleventh and twelfth grades, living in a girls' boardinghouse where the landlady was forever yelling, "You girls, stop walking around in your *underwear*!"

When I told my dad I was going to go for a doctorate, he said, "What took you so long?" as though he'd always expected it of me. He'd worked his way up at the bank from a teller, and I followed his example into the working world. Still, because I was a woman, when I bought my first car, even though I had a job, they made my father co-sign. You couldn't get a credit card in your own name as a woman until 1974! Your husband or your father had to let you have one.

One of the things I loved about Joe was his support of my education. On the day of my graduation for my doctoral degree, he secretly decorated the driveway leading up to our house with signs saying WELCOME HOME, *DR.* BIDEN.

When I saw that as we returned home, I thought two things: One, *I'm a Dr. now!* Two, *I married the right man.*

CHAPTER 9

Current events tend to shape First Ladies' agendas. World War II caused Eleanor Roosevelt to focus on civil defense. In the wake of September 11, Laura Bush began working on behalf of women in Afghanistan. Our era's crisis was COVID, and as a result, I initially spent much of my time as First Lady traveling to schools and hospitals working to help people get vaccinated, and to rebuild trust.

We were tested for COVID every day for three years. During our administration, I contracted the virus four times. Once, as the result of an infection while on the road, I was stuck on Kiawah Island, South Carolina, for two weeks, which sounds like a lot more fun than it was. Every time I got sick, I gave thanks that it wasn't worse and that I was able to stay out of the hospital, where doctors and nurses were overwhelmed, their resources strained to the breaking point.

One of the first orders of business in the administration was to simultaneously take the virus seriously and do everything possible to get life back to normal. The expression of gratitude I heard perhaps more than any other was to thank Joe for a "return to sanity" after so much chaos. That, and that people seemed to appreciate the way Joe showed respect for the nation's grief, and urged us to come together around it, rather than letting it divide us. We believed it was important to pay tribute to the unbearably high and still-growing death toll, and to the more than one hundred thousand people who were hospitalized.

On day two in office, Joe signed ten pandemic-related executive orders. One called for the opening of a hundred new vaccination sites, which had begun giving shots to seniors in January. "We didn't get into this mess overnight, and it is going to take months to get it turned around," he said. His goal was to get one hundred million shots done in a hundred days. He warned that we would likely soon reach the death toll of five hundred thousand Americans lost to COVID, a number Joe and I would mourn alongside Kamala and Doug at a candlelight vigil and moment of silence the following month on the South Portico of the White House. That was a time of so much darkness and so much pain, and it galvanized Joe to act decisively.

As part of the vaccination effort, Chief Medical Advisor Dr. Anthony Fauci and I hit the road together and traveled all over the country. By this point, I was so grateful to be connecting with people in person after so much time apart. Tony was easy to travel with. We had our routine down. I would talk about vaccination from a mother's point of view. He would speak from a medical point of view. We'd explain why vaccines made sense, and we'd encourage people who were being vaccinated. I'd have the patients squeeze my hand if they needed some support. Personally, I'm terrified of needles, but I went to one vaccination clinic after another to get the word out. At a Harlem church, Dr. Fauci and I witnessed shots going into the arms of New Yorkers, from teens to ninety-year-olds.

When Dr. Fauci and I went on *Live with Kelly and Ryan*, Kelly Ripa honored the work of teachers, which, of course, is always a shortcut to my heart. She said, "One of the silver linings of the pandemic was that parents really understood how tough the job of teaching is, because on the other side of the computer is a hapless parent trying to just log their child on."

For our first Valentine's Day in the White House, I wanted to do something cheerful to celebrate the holiday while people were still being kept apart by the pandemic. I drew conversation hearts on a piece of paper and showed the carpentry office. They said they loved the idea and painted late into the night. The next morning, February 12, I told Joe to look out the window. Overnight, giant cutout hearts with phrases like "Unity," "Courage," "Healing," "Kindness," and "Compassion" had appeared on the lawn. The display was signed "Love, Jill."

Joe wanted to go down to look at the hearts close-up, so we took our coffee out on the lawn, where he chatted with reporters. When asked what he would say to Americans who were feeling discouraged almost a year into COVID, he said, "There's hope. You just have to stay strong." He spoke about those who had lost loved ones: "The only thing I can say to them is that they're still in your heart . . . I can tell you from experience, they're in your heart."

Early March 2021 was a liminal time. The vaccine was available, though not yet for everyone, and most people in the country hadn't had their two shots. Masks and capacity limits were still enforced in many places. Facing a third wave, countries in Europe were back on lockdown. Like so many people, Joe and I had cabin fever. And so, one night, with DC traffic stilled by closures and travel bans, I ordered takeout from Le Diplomate and invited Joe to meet me for dinner on the White House grounds, in the tennis pavilion. It was one of those rare moments when we realized that it was really just the two of us on this journey.

The vaccine tours were challenging, but they made me feel like at least there was finally something to do that might help end the devastation of COVID. In Texas, Second Gentleman Doug Emhoff and I went to an Astros game to call attention to a pop-up vaccination clinic at the stadium. With country star Brad Paisley, I visited a clinic that had been set up at a bar. When we had little kids getting shots, we brought in US Surgeon General Vivek Murthy, because he was very good with parents. In that first year, I went to thirty-five states and fifty cities to promote vaccination efforts.

A pandemic should not be politicized. The virus did not care who you voted for. Fewer lives could have been lost if more people had gotten the vaccine—a miracle of modern science that resulted from a bipartisan effort. Some leaders made things worse by spreading fear of the vaccine and discouraging mask-wearing. I tried to remind myself that every one of us shared the same goal: for there to come a day when COVID would become just another annoying flu.

The administration had been pushing for a Summer of Freedom, hoping to get back to some semblance of normalcy by the Fourth of July. At last, we hoped, we could all take off our masks and gather with friends and family to celebrate the country and how we'd made it through the worst days of the pandemic. Well, best-laid plans—the Delta variant showed up with a vengeance and foiled the push for normalcy.

The Summer Olympics in Japan had been rescheduled from the previous year due to COVID. I was invited to lead the US delegation to the games. It was decided that I should go to Japan alone, without the fuller delegation that is customary. That was my first solo foreign trip as First Lady. Because of COVID, the stadiums were nearly empty, lending an eerie quality to the games. I sat twenty feet from French President Emmanuel Macron to watch the US play France in three-on-three basketball. (We won.) How terrible for the athletes to have worked so hard to get there and then not to have their families in the stands. They were resilient, though, or they wouldn't have been Olympians.

On that trip, I dined with Japanese Prime Minister Yoshihide Suga and his wife, Mariko. We talked about COVID and our families while enjoying a dinner of tempura shrimp, scallops, vegetables, two soups, and fruit. Our conversation was comfortable, if somewhat challenging with three interpreters and a plexiglass shield between us.

In Tokyo, we weren't allowed to walk the streets because of the increasing pandemic numbers. I would have loved to have seen the city in some way other than from a car window. Lockdowns had so many of us feeling claustrophobic. I kept tearing down the paper they'd put up to cover the windows of my room at the embassy. I was told it was for my safety, but I wanted to see the sunshine and gardens outside. I wanted those memories of Japan.

I'm grateful that COVID is now nowhere near as lethal as it was. In the US, COVID has indeed become more or less like the flu, with its mortality down from roughly 367,000 deaths in 2020 to around 47,000 in 2024. I give thanks for the clarity and steadfastness Joe brought to that confusing and terrifying time, and to the doctors and scientists who developed a vaccine, and to all those across the country who did their part to get us here.

CHAPTER 10

While the White House is a beautiful landmark, it's the people working there who make it such an incredibly special home. Many of them have been there for decades and take tremendous pride in making the First Family feel cared for, and ensuring that the building's long history is preserved.

When we lived at the residence, as it's affectionately called, there was a constant ebb and flow of people at all hours. Briefing papers were delivered at dawn. I'd awaken looking up at a huge chandelier in the middle of the room, and at one of my favorite paintings, the lush and cheerful *Pennsylvania Peonies*, by Delawarean Mary Page Evans. Most nights, Joe and I would eat dinner in a room called the Yellow Oval, in front of the fireplace.

In the winter, the snowfalls were ethereal when viewed from those big windows in all the rooms. When I returned from teaching, I'd spread a blanket over the radiator covers by the windows in our bedroom. That's where I'd sit to drink tea and write or grade papers. Nobody looking in could see me there because a huge magnolia tree was just outside.

I am always making lists on scraps of paper—holiday shopping lists, to-do lists, grocery lists. I recently found one that I wrote almost twenty years ago in which I listed some of the things I couldn't live without. They included the ocean, the full moon, the warmth of the sun, a view of the lake, my garden, books, my grandchildren laughing, and an animal in the house. To me, a house is not a home without a pet. I think there are pet people and non-pet people; you either love animals or you don't. We're a family that's always had pets.

"That cat thinks she's a dog!" Joe said when I adopted a little gray tabby from a barn in Pennsylvania while out on the campaign trail. Not that I felt I had much say in bringing Willow home—she marched right up and insisted. Full of personality and—Joe was right—a puppy-like confidence, once we were finally able to bring her to the White House, she settled in right away.

Mornings when I went to work, she headed straight to the stairwell and went to spend the day with the people who took care of the house. They had a little bed up there for her and special food dishes and a litter box, and they called her "Willita."

During our time in the White House, I wrote a children's book about Willow—how I came to adopt her, and how she spent her time sleeping in the Oval Office or watching me read to children on the lawn. I loved seeing Willow bring joy to children, just as she brings joy to us.

Flowers have always been an important part of my life, too. I planted a cutting garden at the White House so I could take bouquets to friends or acquaintances who were sick, had suffered the loss of a loved one, or just needed a pick-me-up. My mother always had a simple garden and made it a point to have flowers on the dinner table. I took flower arranging in college as one of my electives. The White House florist, Hedieh Ghaffarian, placed flowers in every room in the most creative, beautiful ways. Sometimes, after a really hard day, I'd find a stunning bouquet by my bed. I prefer low vases with fun mixes of flowers to tight bouquets, so that's what Hedieh would arrange.

The First Lady gets to choose the color of the tulips that surround the White House fountains. I chose different colors each year. In 2023, they were red, pink, and pink-and-white. That same year, the Dutch ambassador presented me with my own namesake flower: a reddish-orange tulip with fringed petals. The tradition of presenting the First Lady with a signature tulip dates back to the late 1800s, with Grover Cleveland's wife, Frances Folsom. At the gifting ceremony held at the Danish embassy, I said, "In this happy time, let these tulips' dazzling orange be a reminder of the many springs our nations have shared."

The ground floor of the White House is where the public tours are held. As a teacher, I knew the tours needed improving when I saw young people zoning out on their phones rather than looking around as they walked through the building. For starters, I swapped out some of the nineteenth-century presidential portraits and moved some more recent portraits of contemporary First Ladies, people who guests would know, into the public spaces.

Then I worked with the History Channel, the National Park Service, the White House Historical Association, and ESI Design, an immersive design firm, to change the White House visit experience from a traditional walk-through tour to an interactive educational one. I know that learning involves multisensory elements, so I wanted to incorporate the senses of sight, sound, and touch. I thought it was important that the tone be warm and inviting from beginning to end.

We created an architectural model of the White House and used it to explain the ways in which the building had evolved from its inception. The Diplomatic Reception Room was now included on the tour. Its walls are covered with a French panorama wallpaper called *Les vues d'Amérique du Nord* ("Views of North America") that dates back to 1834. It was installed in 1961 by Jacqueline Kennedy as part of her effort to decorate the White House with scenes designed to make Americans feel proud of their shared history.

Rather than just a tour guide mentioning FDR's fireside chats, an old radio played his addresses in a room where you could actually touch the marble of the fireplace. In the new tour, guests could go farther into the rooms instead of just peering through a crowded doorway. We changed the stationary pictures in the East Wing colonnade to digital ones. Every few moments, the screen would show a new scene from the life of a presidential family. It was much more dynamic.

I tried to warm up our private spaces, too. Upstairs, I hung family photos and some of the grandchildren's art—Maisy is an incredibly talented visual artist—on white linen painter's cloth, added wallpaper, and brought in a small forest's worth of plants. I also tried to liven up the art on display, because many of the paintings had been in the same place so long that their identifying name plates were scuffed to the point that you could hardly read them.

With the help of my friend Ellen Susman, the former director of the Art in Embassies program, I put together a collection with work loaned by the Hirshhorn, the National Gallery, and individuals who told us they were honored to be included. I hung work by artists like Mark Rothko, Alex Katz, Hans Hofmann, Ellsworth Kelly, and Sylvia Plimack Mangold.

The first time I saw the dining room, I gasped. "The Diebenkorn and Albers really make the room sing," Ellen said.

My East Wing office felt like no other part of the White House. Our granddaughter Finnegan had suggested asking the designer Mark D. Sikes to help make it feel both elegant and cozy. We put in blue-and-white-striped silk fabric, and I added a portrait of the family taken by Annie Leibovitz alongside the grandkids' artwork. Natalie and Little Hunter had painted self-portraits in their high school art classes and given them to me as Christmas gifts. An artist named Terry Romero Paul had sent me an oil painting of the army boots Beau had worn in Iraq. Hunter gave me my favorite painting of his one year for Christmas, a bird in shades of blue. It was the focal point of the room as you walked through the doors.

To bring nature inside, there were ficus trees in the corners and flowers on the tables. My office looked out over the Jacqueline Kennedy Garden. I couldn't thank the National Parks Service enough for tending to the grounds with such loving care. The flower beds were breathtaking in any season. I'd often meet with friends or staff in the white gazebo there.

My bookshelves were filled with books given to me by authors Ann Patchett, Barbara Kingsolver, and Jesmyn Ward; the White House Historical Association; and others. Several items of interest—White House–themed Easter eggs, a piece of shrapnel from the war in Ukraine, baskets given to me by Native Americans—adorned the shelves. Ginger-lemon tea with honey—or something harder—was available on my tea cart for guests.

I always looked forward to working there with my staff around a long rectangular table or settled into my comfortable blue velvet couch or chairs. I wanted my guests to feel welcome, and I wanted my staff to feel as though we were in a place where everyone's opinions were welcome.

First Ladies usually take a few months to assemble their senior staff. Mine was ready to go on day one: Julissa Reynoso Pantaleón was my chief of staff. Carlos Elizondo was my social secretary. Mala Adiga was my policy director. Elizabeth Alexander was my communications director. Anthony Bernal, who had been with me since 2008, continued to hold us all together.

We all felt the gravity of the office, and no one took it for granted. Working at the White House is all-consuming. We knew one another's families and the daily stresses caused by the complexity of the job, definitely not a nine-to-five. Often, someone would call me at six in the morning or ten at night. We had lots of early-morning flights and late-evening events. But we all felt a sense of purpose in the work we were doing, whether it was providing jobs for military spouses, lifting up teachers, offering patient navigators to cancer patients and their families, or promoting research for women's health.

If a colleague had to call me late in the day because they were finishing up work after putting their children to bed, I understood. I was a working mom for many years. You have to know how and when you can write that memo or shoot off a response. You've got to grab those moments. We formed a family. I respected them all for the breadth of their knowledge, their savvy. Everyone brought something different to the table. No one complained. We were ordinary people living extraordinary lives, and that honor was not lost on us.

The White House staff made it their business to know what you liked. After an event, I would usually come upstairs and have a glass of cabernet, so there would always be one waiting for me. When our family would come for a visit, I made sure that everybody had cookies. They loved the White House cookies—chocolate chip or glazed white to look like the White House or in colors to imitate fall leaves. One of my sisters likes cream in her coffee rather than milk, so without even being asked, they'd have half-and-half in the refrigerator when she visited. Whatever you wanted, the kitchen would make for you. If you called down at eleven o'clock at night and you wanted a cheeseburger, you could get it.

The staff would create the ambiance that you wanted. So if you enjoyed jazz and a martini, that's what you'd arrive home to. Joe was always within arm's reach of a Coke Zero or an ice cream bar. His closet was like an Excel spreadsheet—perfectly straight lines of white shirts, blue shirts. Shoes shined every day.

To perform at the People's House is a distinct honor, and we tried to give that opportunity to as many different groups and individuals as possible. Finnegan suggested we bring the Philadelphia Eagles singing trio, the Philly Specials, to the White House, which was *great*. I am a die-hard Eagles fan. Fly, Eagles, fly!

Elton John also came to give a concert. The day before, his band had a practice session with a soundalike (was that possible?) singer. I was upstairs in the residence when I heard that familiar banging on the piano . . . you know those chords that begin “Bennie and the Jets”? I raced downstairs. It all felt so exciting. They were doing the soundcheck and rehearsing. There we were—the staff running to sit in the seats and watch.

The concert itself was magnificent, with a gorgeous glass canopy above our heads. That night, Joe gave Elton an arts and humanities award. He has done so much to promote AIDS awareness. He’s truly one of a kind—a special human being.

I loved when the Kennedy Center honorees came to the White House. The 2021 group included Dick Van Dyke, Garth Brooks, Debbie Allen, and Joan Baez. After pictures were taken, Joan Baez spontaneously broke into the civil rights anthem “Ain’t Gonna Let Nobody Turn Me ’Round,” changing some of the words to be about Joe saving the country and giving people hope. Debbie harmonized while Garth and his wife, country singer Trisha Yearwood, hummed along.

U2’s Bono, my longtime crush, habitually breaks into poetry as part of conversation. Joe’s favorite poet is Seamus Heaney, so when we’ve spent time with Bono, he’s peppered conversation with lines like “All year the flax-dam festered in the heart . . .” If you think a rock star spouting poetry from memory would not make an English teacher swoon, *you would be wrong.*

One year, for my birthday, friends took me to the Sphere to see U2. You can’t really describe the Sphere to someone. You have to experience it—full immersion: seeing, feeling, hearing. The best part of the night was when Bono dedicated “All I Want Is You” to “all the great women in our lives” and name-checked me—or was the best part getting to join the prayer circle backstage with the band and their families? It was certainly a birthday I’ll never forget.

Opening the White House wider and wider to more people mattered to me. Sometimes events would also yield remarkable friendships.

"You remind me of my wife, Ricky," Ralph Lauren said one day. She and I gravitated toward each other at a White House event and formed an instant connection.

As a rule, I preferred less buzz around me rather than more. I was successful in my bid to do away with the tradition of having an usher ride in the elevator with me to push the button, for example. Each day before I went to work, I'd head to the kitchen to make my own coffee—it's best for everyone if I'm alone before I've had caffeine. I bought a purple lunch bag, and one of the treats of the White House was having salads packed for my school lunches. Those little rituals simulated normalcy—even though nothing about living in the White House is normal.

CHAPTER 11

There's an aura of mystery around the other presidential residence, Camp David. While it feels like a vacation home, with its dozen cabins in the Catoctin Mountain Park of Maryland, about sixty miles from DC, it's actually a United States naval installation. FDR called it Shangri-La; then Eisenhower renamed it Camp David in honor of his father and grandson. Ronald Reagan spent the most time there of all the presidents, with a remarkable 189 visits.

Nestled in the woods, the cabins, built from 1935 to 1938 during the FDR administration, are warm, cozy, and peaceful. Our grandkids especially loved their time at Camp David—the pool, the gym, the tennis courts, the putting green, the movie theater, the clay pigeon shooting range. There was so much to do! There are wooded paths for bikes and golf carts. Every family member was assigned a golf cart with their name on the front, and it was one of the few times during the presidency that the Secret Service let Joe and me drive ourselves.

The main presidential cabin is called Aspen Lodge, and the largest structure is the dining cabin, Laurel Lodge. In the winter, it did get cold, so we'd always have the fireplaces going. In the summers, the family would gather around the pool in Aspen's backyard. The kids loved to go in the arcade and gift shop. There's even a bar on-site with lots of fun snacks and bar food. Every trip, we stocked up on Camp David merch at the gift shop—wineglasses, T-shirts, pajamas.

We let the kids choose what movies to watch in the theater, and the staff would make sure there was plenty of popcorn and candy. We'd snuggle in the big reclining armchairs, covered by blankets bearing the name of Joe's administration. At night, we could enjoy s'mores at the outdoor firepit or sit and look up at the stars. It was so dark there that on a clear night you could see many more stars than back home.

Camp David included a chapel, where the military was invited to attend—and there would always be homemade cookies by the door. They had several services, from Protestant to Catholic to nondenominational, and different pastors, ministers, and priests were invited to give sermons. Music was part of every service, and the military members played the piano and sang. The bell would be rung when the president entered.

But the best part—by far—was the military staff. The staff seemed to recognize the enormity of the job of being president and to take great pride in giving Joe—and, by extension, his family—a place to decompress. They would prepare for weeks for one of our visits, making everything special for us. I'd send up menu suggestions, and they would shop, prepare, and serve us breakfast, lunch, and dinner. They had all our favorite family meals down: chicken parmesan and pasta, blueberry pancakes, soup and sandwiches. Of course there was *always* ice cream.

We usually flew to Camp David by helicopter. The military, along with the admiral, would be there to greet us on arrival and bid us farewell on departure. We got to personally know so many of the military members. We knew where they were from, if they were single or married, and their life ambitions.

We'd walk into Aspen Lodge to the sound of our favorite music playing softly in the background. The fire would barely be dying down when the staff would appear with an armful of logs. *Would you like lemonade or sangria at the pool? Need a birthday cake? No problem.* (I never could get the TV to work, but that was entirely on me because I was too embarrassed to admit it had stumped me.) There's a medical unit and also a fully manned fire station. A barbershop is available if you need a haircut.

The tone of every interaction I had at Camp David: *Relax. We're here to take care of you.* That's what they did. They created a welcome space for the family to do as much or as little as we wanted.

I loved waking up early in the morning to watch the sun rise over the mountains as the mist dissipated. I'd just sit and drink my coffee before Joe got up or the kids came down to get something from the fridge. Aspen had everything you could want for a vacation house—though I went to do some laundry one day and was told that a prior resident had removed the washer and dryer. I asked that it be reinstalled.

Oh, and the flowers! Fresh bouquets were sent from the White House, so the rooms of our cabins were fragrant with blooms. The Camp David staff planted the sloping hill in the backyard with all the colors of the season. I marveled at the hours and hours it must have taken to fill the window boxes and all those flower beds.

Outside of Aspen Lodge is a koi pond, and even in winter, you can see the fish. There is fish food hanging in a container so you can feed them morning and night. The pond was originally put in as a water source near the president's cabin, as the cabins are wood and they wanted it to be protected in case of fire.

During the July 2024 NATO summit, I hosted an informal lunch at Camp David for the dozens of spouses of the leaders attending. I encouraged everyone to dress casually. Before each event, I received dossiers of material to read in preparation. My NATO briefing book—which included bios of everyone attending, along with reminders of how to address them and where we'd met before—was 175 pages long. I had a feeling my fellow spouses were as eager for a day off as I was.

Our day began with a helicopter ride from DC into Camp David. There were cocktails and classical music in the gazebo. We served lobster crepes on the patio. Then the visitors went on history tours of the complex, and I took it as a sign of enthusiasm that, before they left, just about everyone loaded up on Camp David–branded merch at the gift shop.

Spending Easter at Camp David was one of my favorite traditions. I dyed the eggs the night before Easter (usually forgetting to add the vinegar), and Joe hid them. We also filled some plastic eggs with money, to entice even the older kids to partake in the hunt. Somewhere in the yard behind Aspen sits a plastic Easter egg with a ten-dollar bill inside. I wonder if it will ever be found. We only spent one Christmas there as a family, in 2023, but it was a good one, with all the kids and grandkids piling into our cabin wearing their pajamas.

Camp David was a place to renew and reflect. The air was so clean and pure. It always took a minute for Joe to unwind, but eventually he'd give in and put aside his briefing books for a moment. I feel so much gratitude to our military for taking such good care of our nation every day and of my family on those too-rare trips.

CHAPTER 12

Privacy is scarce when you're First Lady. Very little happens without lots of people knowing. I'd get a call from my personal aide, Jordan Montoya, saying, "How much longer will you be at the doctor?" I'd say, "How do you know I'm at the doctor? Do you have me chipped?"

My every movement was tracked by Secret Service and made available to staff via radio. I found it hard to get used to constantly being monitored. I thought I knew about what it meant to have Secret Service protection, but the First Lady has a much bigger detail than the Second Lady.

Your code name is chosen when you come into protection. They give you a letter from the alphabet and let you choose your word. Our letter was *C*. Joe came up with Celtic because he's Irish. I became Capri because my family's from Italy. The grandkids had cute names like Cookie, Coaster, and Cowboy.

Every bit of mail you received—your bank statement, a letter from your grandmother—all of it was opened for security reasons. The constant attention made little escapes feel luxurious. One beautiful, hot summer night, Joe was away, but Naomi and Ashley were around, and someone said, "Let's go to the top of the White House!" Giggling with childlike freedom, we clambered onto the roof—and kept climbing until we were on the walkway where the sharpshooters with their long guns usually stationed themselves. The view was spectacular, and it felt like such a treat to be out there.

When we went out on the Truman balcony off the Yellow Oval, a buzzer rang downstairs, which meant they'd have to clear President's Park, known as the Ellipse. I was told that the protocol was put in place because during the Obama administration, someone had shot at the White House from there, and it hit right by their bedroom window. When the weather was nice, we'd long to have dinner out on the balcony, but we only did that rarely because we knew that if we did, hundreds of tourists would be asked to clear the area.

There are layers of Secret Service, including the CAT squad, the "counter assault team" sharpshooters who are often hidden on rooftops and in trees. They're a special division of the Secret Service. They look like they're made out of bricks, and you can't miss them with their dark glasses and gear. They're extremely impressive, and that includes the about one in four Secret Service agents who are women.

We also had specialists, so if you were skiing, you'd have an agent who was an expert skier. Same with biking, swimming. There'd be a frogman in the water if Joe went to the beach. You also had K-9 units. Bomb-sniffing dogs would check out just about any room we entered. They'd run through my school before I taught, into the nail salon before I got a manicure, into my workout studio before a barre or cycle class, all over my hotel room before I went inside.

If we traveled by car, the roads and bridges would be shut down to let us through. The state police and the local police would coordinate it. It took me a long time to get used to that. When they drove us through, they'd ignore traffic lights, and every time we came up to a red light, I'd press my foot down on an imaginary brake to stop. When I wound up without a driver again after eight years as Second Lady, I had to learn everything about driving again. Until I got back into the habit, I found it scary, especially on I-95.

When you have protection, being spontaneous is difficult. During the White House years, Joe also had a press corps, so you'd have to coordinate with them if you were going to do anything. If we were going to walk down the street to the beach, we'd have to let the press know so they could cover that movement.

Being First Lady could feel like a catch-22. You were encouraged to use your platform to do good, but not to be too aggressive in pursuing policy goals, lest you be seen as overreaching. If you knew too little about what you were talking about, then you were an embarrassment. If you knew too much, you were trying to rule the world.

At White House and international events, there were more moments of confusing protocol than I can count, instances of *Wait, did he not shake my hand on purpose?* Or *Was I supposed to exit stage right?* When it came to my clothes, the scrutiny was relentless. Once, in 2021, I wore a green knit dress with a leather hem, paired with patterned black tights. I had allegedly been wearing fishnets and therefore been dressing too provocatively. To me, they were just pretty lace stockings. Another time, I used a scrunchie to pull back my hair, which resulted in a deluge of commentary. This was on the way to Camp David; I'd stopped at a bakery to pick up brownies and cupcakes for Valentine's Day.

Perhaps most dramatically, in October 2022, I was accused of having dressed down Joe's staff earlier that year. Joe was downstairs doing a news conference while I was upstairs watching on live TV. The questions kept coming, and he kept answering them, and time kept rolling on—half an hour, an hour, an hour and a half . . . I'd go do something and come back, and he was still answering questions.

People at home, I was sure, had long since stopped watching. It's traditionally somebody's job to step up to the podium and say, "Thank you, Mr. President." But no one did. The Q&A went on and on for nearly two hours, to the point of absurdity. When it finally came to a close—probably because the journalists had all run out of ink in their pens and space in their notebooks—I went over to the Treaty Room, where the staff had gathered. "Whose responsibility is it to stop it, because he will go on forever?" I said.

There's long been a fear of the First Lady because she's the closest person to the president, and everyone recognizes that, so I usually kept my thoughts to myself. On that day, though, I said what I thought. My question leaked to the press—and there it was: another bad news day I hadn't seen coming.

CHAPTER 13

My office was located in the White House's East Wing—may it rest in peace. Every day, I traversed the downstairs hallway, past portraits of the former First Ladies. I glanced at each image, particularly the more recent ones. It was a humbling reminder that I was now part of a relatively small group of American women who'd called this place home and been charged with its preservation.

In early April 2022, I held an informal meeting in the Blue Room with seven First Lady historians. I wanted to hear about Eleanor Roosevelt's writing, Betty Ford's support of the ERA, and Nancy Reagan's war on drugs. I was also able to learn about the formation of an organization at American University's School of Public Affairs called FLARE (First Ladies Association for Research and Education), the first association dedicated to the study of America's First Ladies. The historians helped me think more deeply about this special role.

The symbolism and style of each portrait interested me. Some First Ladies included their pets, like Grace Coolidge, who stands in a striking red dress beside her white collie, Rob Roy. Eleanor Roosevelt's portrait has no discernible background as she looks directly at the viewers. Her portrait is unique in that the lower part of the frame shows her in various roles. All the choices are deliberate and need to withstand the test of time. Jacqueline Kennedy looks away and slightly downward. Her portrait, which was painted several years after President Kennedy's death, is haunting—you can read the grief in her demeanor.

The First Lady who made the biggest impression on me when I was a young girl was, of course, Jackie. JFK's assassination took place when I was in eighth grade. It was a Friday. They called us into the school auditorium and told us, then sent us home. We were all glued to the TV for days. I actually saw Jack Ruby shoot Lee Harvey Oswald live on television. Americans loved John and Jackie and their beautiful young children. I admired her, and, along with everyone else I knew, I grieved the loss of the president as if he were a member of my own family.

About fifteen years later, the night after Joe and I got married at the United Nations chapel in New York, we took the boys to see *Annie* on Broadway. There we encountered Jackie with her then partner, Maurice Tempelsman, a few rows behind us on the aisle. We excitedly whispered to the boys that she was there, but at seven and eight, they didn't yet know who she was or her part in history.

When we got to the White House, I could still see her influence, from the wallpaper in the Diplomatic Reception Room to seasonal flowers in the gardens.

In Betty Ford's portrait, she wears a pale blue dress and looks out of the frame with warmth and compassion. I came to profoundly admire her as First Lady, because she was so open and honest about having breast cancer and later her battle with addiction. She heroically discussed her alcoholism, easing the stigma and helping countless people get into treatment.

In her portrait, Barbara Bush focuses straight at the viewer. This directness was part of her character, and the pearls around her neck were part of her signature style. Barbara Bush might have looked grandmotherly, but she was nobody's fool. The portrait captures her strength, and yet also shows her soft side—her beloved dog Millie appears with her, a tribute to her love of animals. Her grandchildren seemed to adore her, which is usually a pretty good measure of character.

Laura Bush's portrait reflects her quiet, serene side. The painting's setting is the Green Room, which was restored under her direction during her husband's administration. It meant so much to me when, in the spirit of putting the country before party, Laura invited me to sit at her table at a White House Senate spouses' luncheon. This was leading up to the 2004 presidential race, when it was rumored that Joe might run. I was delighted to get to know a fellow book lover, and I told her that I so admired the work she did promoting libraries.

Laura was much quieter than her gregarious husband, but she has a fun-loving side, and I imagine she must laugh a lot with George. I also got the sense that they had a romantic marriage. One time, I was meeting with President Bush at the George W. Bush Library after speaking to military families there. Laura came in and said, "Hey, Bushy," then sauntered into the hallway for a cup of coffee as he smiled after her.

Hillary Clinton's portrait shows her smiling broadly in a black pantsuit, one hand on a chair and the other on a table. I often paused to look at this painting on my walks because I was truly amazed by Hillary Clinton as First Lady. She hosted a fundraiser for Joe in 1996, when he was running to hold on to his Senate seat. Wearing a beautiful brown St. John knit pantsuit, she spoke at first from a podium and then came and spoke to what felt like every single person in the room one-on-one. I was so impressed by how she was able to instantly change topics and speak with such insight on each of them. She must have an encyclopedic memory.

Hillary and Joe ran against each other in the 2008 presidential election. (It was supposed to be "her year," but then Barack Obama won the Iowa caucus.) When Barack was assembling his cabinet, Joe supported her for secretary of state. She and Joe had a good working relationship, having spent eight years together in the Senate. Once Joe became president, we started inviting the Clintons to the White House. I saw her in a different way—as one of the greatest politicians of our time, as well as a singularly kind person. She'd say, "Anything I can help you with, call me," and she meant it.

I don't think you ever really know who your friends are going to be until things get rough and they stick around. As Dr. Martin Luther King Jr. said: "The world is all messed up. The nation is sick. Trouble is in this land; confusion all around . . . But I know, somehow, that only when it is dark enough can you see the stars."

In 2024, Hillary and Bill stuck with us through the entirety of the hard summer. Hillary had been through so much and seemed to have gained deep knowledge and grace as a result. I felt very lucky that she was willing to share it with me.

When Joe decided to get out of the race in 2024, we had them come to dinner to talk about the afterlife—what they did, what mistakes they felt they'd made, setting up their foundation, giving speeches. They left the White House when they were in their fifties, and Joe and I were much older, so our situation was different. Still, they had a lot of wisdom to share.

After that, Hillary and I made plans for time alone, and we had tea for about three hours. The relationship blossomed into something meaningful. Hillary and Bill ended up being good friends.

Interestingly, Hillary chose to put several elements of her life into her official White House portrait. She stands confidently in the Blue Room in front of the fireplace mantel. On the table beside her is her book *It Takes a Village* and her White House china.

Michelle Obama's portrait is striking—you can't walk by and not stop to gaze. She chose to be seated on a couch in the Red Room wearing a powder blue gown, with a peach-colored background in a similar hue as her White House offices. It captures her beautifully—she exudes calm and confidence. The Obamas added their portraits to the White House collection during Joe's administration. Michelle and Barack; Michelle's mother, Marian; and Marian's friend Mama Kaye joined us for lunch upstairs in the Yellow Oval before going downstairs to greet their friends and family for the official unveiling.

It remains to be seen how such things will be handled going forward. While the portrait gallery might seem like a small thing, I've been dismayed by some of the changes to tradition. And yet, as Robert Frost wrote in a short poem in 1923:

So Eden sank to grief,
So dawn goes down to day.
Nothing gold can stay.

The call to put political differences aside for the greater good is on display nowhere more so than in the traditions surrounding transitions of power. My first experience of such a ceremony was our transition tea with Dick and Lynne Cheney at Number One Observatory Circle, the vice president's home.

No sooner had Lynne poured the ceremonial tea than they both jumped up and said, "Let us show you the house!" I'd just begun to raise the cup to my lips for a first sip. I hastily set it down so I could follow them out the door. Joe and I trailed behind the Cheneys as they speed-walked us from room to room.

The press was summoned for a departure photo. Waving, Dick and Lynne called out, "Goodbye! Nice of you to come!" as they led us to our car.

The whole thing seemed like it lasted maybe fifteen minutes. The ceremonial tea was probably still hot. Driving away, Joe and I couldn't stop laughing. "Were we even there?" he said.

Those tours are an important part of the peaceful transition of power in a democracy. They can also be phenomenally awkward. Tough words can be exchanged during campaigns, but you show up as a sign of unity. All the while, the press has bright lights shining on your front door. They're reading motives into every aspect of the interaction.

In January 2017, it was our turn to host. Mike and Karen Pence came to the vice president's residence for lunch. We placed a small table in the sunroom for just the four of us. I wanted them to love this house as much as we did. Joe told Mike that he would be available to him 24/7. I thought the meeting went really well, and I was pleased when Mike told the press that he and Karen felt the same way.

Afterward, Karen gave me a painting of the residence that she had painted herself. It now hangs in our Wilmington home at the top of the stairway—a daily reminder to me that politics can be civil.

Even before you leave the White House, the curators and White House Historical Association ask you to start planning your White House portraits. Which artist will you select? What room will you choose? What will you wear? Would you like to stage photographs for the artist to use? I started taking photos to remember the details of the rooms and spaces I loved, but it all felt a bit overwhelming and wasn't something I could focus on in those final days.

Choosing a portrait artist is a process. White House archivists gave me several suggestions, as did the National Portrait Gallery. I've since spent hours looking at books, and I visited the National Portrait Gallery exhibition. I narrowed down my choices and then interviewed several people. I chose David Larned because I felt he captured his subjects with authenticity, and also because he is a Delawarean.

Will I wear a blue dress—or maybe a suit? I'd like the image to reflect my independence. I want people to feel like they know me. I hope I remind them of their English teacher, their mom, their sister, their best friend—approachable yet reserved, confident, maybe a hint of mischief behind my smile.

CHAPTER 14

My husband has always said that all politics is personal. This is evident on the international stage. The partners of world leaders share an understanding because of our common role, and protocol often requires hosting each other for anything from a casual tea at home to an elaborate state visit. Trips abroad weren't always easy given my teaching schedule, but I made them a priority and was rewarded with a number of close relationships. Spending time with fellow First Spouses provided me with an education in the histories and traditions of other cultures, as well as in human nature.

The first world leader's spouse to visit the White House after COVID restrictions were lifted was Queen Rania of Jordan, who came with her husband in July 2021. She and I wound up spending a good deal of time together because Joe had a special relationship with King Abdullah II, dating back to when Joe was a senator and Abdullah was a prince. In 2016, Joe, Hallie, Natalie, and I went to see them along with Beau's son, Hunter, who turned ten on that trip. The royal family often traveled with their four children, so they knew just how to make the visit special; they served him a giant chocolate birthday cake. The next year, Joe had the king at our beach house for hamburgers. Wearing a long champagne-colored Reem Acra dress, I attended the Jordanian crown prince's wedding in 2023. As a mother, I knew the joy Rania felt on the occasion of her son's marriage.

Rania and I bonded over advocacy for the education of all children. She told me about her country's successes finding space for migrants at Jordanian schools. When hundreds of thousands of Syrians arrived in Jordan, fleeing ISIS and civil war, some schools became so crowded that there weren't enough places to put students. Maha Salim Al-Ashqar, principal of a girls' primary school there, was not daunted. As I understood it, she would take any girl who could bring her own chair, and the next day, there was a line of women standing there holding chairs to donate for the little girls.

Beatriz Gutiérrez Müller of Mexico came to the White House for Cinco de Mayo in 2022. While there, she took a Virgin de Guadalupe medallion off from her neck and put it on mine. She'd had my name etched into the back of it, which I found so thoughtful. When I brought her in to say hello to Joe, they wound up talking for an hour.

On her next visit, in July of that year, Beatriz said, "I want you to show me something that nobody else sees." It was a fun request. She was a professor, so I called up the Library of Congress and said, "Let's wow her."

The librarians did an incredible job. They pulled out rare artifacts, some of them significant to Mexico–US relations and Spanish-language literature, and others of historical import: an 1837 Mexican cookbook, an anti-Napoleonic satire from 1809, a second-century papyrus fragment of the *Iliad*, a Gutenberg Bible.

Beatriz seemed genuinely moved by the gesture. She spent time asking questions and discovering the origin and history of every piece. The staff was delighted, of course. This was their forte. Carla Hayden and her librarians went above and beyond in displaying their deep knowledge about the history of Mexico.

Beatriz, who knew I taught writing, hosted me for a celebration of the written word. The event touched my heart. In my remarks, I said, "Art is powerful. Poetry and prose, dance and music—they can unite us across time, and languages, and borders. They show us that our differences are precious and our similarities infinite."

International summits were often a time for First Spouse gatherings. In October 2021, during the G20 Summit in Rome, I had tea with Maria Serenella Cappello, the wife of Italian Prime Minister Mario Draghi, while he and Joe discussed transatlantic security. She kept a low public profile but had agreed to see me, perhaps because she has a degree in English literature and knew we'd have plenty to talk about. We had interpreters, but she didn't need one for our visit. She understood a lot of English, and right away, we *clicked*. It might have been that we were both in our seventies, but in no time, we were just two women swapping stories. She laughed charmingly. She was so open and vulnerable.

I asked her if her husband danced.

She said he "danced like a horse," but she then corrected herself: "I meant, like a bear."

I said, "Well, then my husband dances like the horse."

That G20 trip to Rome was also the first time I met France's First Lady Brigitte Macron. We shared champagne and french fries and talked as if we'd known each other forever. She grew up with three sisters, and she behaved toward me with as much care as if we were family. When our lunch concluded, I walked her over to the press and described us as "two friends together, just like sisters!"

Every time I saw Brigitte, I liked her even more.

When the Macrons were in DC for the state visit in December 2022, I took Brigitte to a museum of language called Planet Word. Alongside a visiting class from a French immersion school, we listened to beautiful poems by Poet Laureate of the United States Ada Limón and former National Student Poet Maya Salameh. I thanked everyone, and Brigitte offered brief remarks in English. She told a parable of two beggars: One holds up a sign that reads BLIND; the other, THE SPRING IS ARRIVING AND I WILL NEVER SEE IT. The second beggar, she explained to the students, received far more charity from passersby, because with his poetry, he was able to help them empathize with his experience: The world will be blooming into color and light, and this man will be left in the dark.

She ended her talk by saying, "We are friends," and she took my hand.

"We are friends," I said, holding her hand as we smiled out at the bright students who'd come to the museum that day to learn about poetry.

Brigitte behaved toward me with great kindness at every turn. I arrived in Paris for the 2024 Summer Olympics opening ceremonies in the middle of a torrential downpour. Before I had to face the public, Brigitte called me into a room she'd saved just for me, and brought in a hair dryer so I could dry off and fix my makeup before I had to greet everyone else.

At the reopening of the Cathedral of Notre Dame in December

2024, after its restoration following the terrible fire that partly destroyed it in 2019, I arrived at my seat and was pleased to find that Brigitte would be by my side. Before she arrived, the US president-elect leaned over to speak to me.

"I had a good meeting with your husband in the Oval Office," he said.

"Yes," I said, "because you're both talkers."

We both laughed. Cameras clicked. The next day, he posted a photo of us as an ad for his cologne, Fight Fight Fight, priced at $199, tagline: "A fragrance your enemies can't resist!"

Really?

In May 2022, I took a four-day trip alone to Eastern Europe to call attention to the humanitarian crisis caused by Russia's Ukraine invasion. On that trip, Romania's First Spouse Carmen Iohannis and I visited a school in Bucharest attended by a group of Ukrainian refugee children. The teacher had written a welcome message to us on the blackboard, and we got to interact with the children around a lesson. Afterward, Carmen cooked me an amazing lunch at her home—Italian food, in honor of my heritage—and then took me for a walk in the gardens by her home, where we talked about everything from our exercise regimens to Shakespeare.

At a White House reception that same month to mark the bicentennial of the Greek War of Independence, I met Mareva Grabowski-Mitsotakis, First Lady of Greece. She had included her daughters, Sofia and Dafni, in our meeting, so Mareva and I bonded as mothers. I later sent cookies to Dafni's Yale dorm her freshman year to help make her feel welcome in the United States. Mareva and I would seek each other out during conferences or meetings, even if only for a quick hello and hug. She invited me to visit her in Greece in the summer, but the timing never worked out.

I traveled to Africa five times as Second Lady. In 2010, I accompanied Joe to Kenya, where I visited a boarding school for orphans while Joe met with the country's leaders to discuss their shared pursuit of peace in the region. Touring the impoverished informal settlement Kibera, I became friendly with a tour guide named Aliyah. When I went back to Kenya many years later, we met up in Kibera. Her toddler had become a teenager, and she had another child, age two. Our reunion was warm, and I was thrilled to see how well she seemed. To me, showing up matters, and showing up again matters more.

I was lucky enough to return to Africa as First Lady in February 2023, bringing my granddaughter Naomi on a trip to Kenya and Namibia (which no American First Lady had visited before). The prior December, I'd hosted twenty-one spouses to presidents of sub-Saharan African nations at the Kennedy Center for the Performing Arts to discuss global cancer prevention and treatment. That was part of where my great affection for Namibia's First Lady Monica Geingos began. She was warm and friendly, and I truly valued her friendship. There were a lot of reasons to go—USAID, the education programs, and using soft diplomacy to remind countries that the United States is a valuable friend.

During Australia's October 2023 state visit, I was speaking with Jodie Haydon, partner of the Australian prime minister, Anthony Albanese, about how our feet were killing us. There had been a great deal of standing and walking that day. I knew that Jodie had walked from Blair House and was going to walk back that night, so before she left, I made sure to track down some sneakers for her to wear home. It's just across the street, but in high heels at the end of a long day, that walk can feel like miles.

Joe and I truly enjoyed their visit to the White House. The day before the state dinner, we did the formal gift exchange and the signing of the official book, and then we sat in the Green Room for a meal together. Because they were English speakers, there was no need for interpreters, so it was just the four of us. It was my first time meeting them. Conversation flowed. They were easy and they seemed like such a good couple. In November 2025, I was delighted by the news that they'd gotten married.

When I first visited First Lady Sophie Grégoire Trudeau in Canada in 2023, she threw a special lunch for me—just the two of us, with flowers and candles—at the National Gallery of Canada in Ottawa. Sophie was fun and energetic, and I was impressed by the way she was working through her writing and speaking to destigmatize mental illness. So when in April 2024 she published a powerful and inspirational memoir called *Closer Together*, I wanted to help her in her work as much as I could. The White House lawyers felt that it would be a violation of the rules against commercial promotion if I threw Sophie a book party, but I invited her to stay as my guest in the Queens' Bedroom, my favorite guest suite. I also stopped by her book talk at Vital Voices Global Headquarters to give some introductory remarks before Huma

Abedin, a political force in her own right, took over as moderator for the evening. I stayed to listen to Sophie's sage advice on the issue of mental health.

Sheikha Moza of Qatar I found to be both one of the most glamorous women in the world and a powerhouse when it comes to providing education to children in need through her foundation Education Above All. In December 2024, Ashley and I—along with my friend Ghada Irani, whom I met through the White House Historical Association—were honored to attend the royal wedding of Sheikha Moza's youngest son at Al Wajba Palace, to which I wore a long beaded Oscar de la Renta gown that shaded from pale blue to a dark floral, as if it represented the sky and the earth. During that trip, I also had the opportunity to visit hospitals and look at different health care systems. What the sheikha has achieved in women's health is both inspiring and impressive. I can see why so many doctors are gravitating toward the research being done and the progress being achieved in Qatar.

One of my favorite moments with a First Couple took place in July 2021, when Germany's Chancellor Angela Merkel and her husband, chemistry professor Joachim Sauer, came to a small dinner in the Blue Room. Chancellor Merkel grew up in East Germany—as did Joachim, by whom she seemed perennially amused. You could tell the two of them had fun. They were always together. It was a true partnership.

Before the dinner, Angela and Joachim joined Joe and me for cocktails upstairs.

Chancellor Merkel said, "Do you still have that Monet?"

"I don't have a Monet," I said. "I think I would know if I had a Monet."

She said, "Well, Joachim and I were here once and President Trump said, 'Do you want to come see my Monet?'" He'd showed it to them. I hadn't even known such a thing was in the building.

So the four of us went on an expedition. Sure enough, in the room off of our bedroom, the big hallway, we had two couches facing each other, and then chairs, and then a big palladium window. The plaques underneath the paintings in our room were small and scratched, and I never looked at them closely. There it was: *Morning on the Seine, Good Weather*, a gold-framed oil painting of the river surrounded by trees, the light soft. I later learned that two weeks after the death of JFK, Jackie Kennedy chose the painting to be a part of the White House's permanent collection in honor of her husband. She put it in the Green Room, President Kennedy's favorite part of the State Floor.

That night we discovered it, the four of us—two world leaders and their partners, and yet also just two couples having drinks during an impromptu house tour—stood back and admired this peaceful, luminous painting belonging to the American people and hanging on the White House wall decade after decade. Our Monet.

CHAPTER 15

The international trips I took were planned well in advance, with every detail accounted for, but many of my domestic trips as First Lady were rapidly arranged visits in response to national tragedies. Whenever something horrific happened, I felt called there as a representative of the country, to show people they were not alone. Steeled for scenes of pain and misery, I would arrive to find wreckage still smoking, floodwaters still receding, grief still raw. From Nashville, Tennessee, to mourn the victims of a school shooting, I would head to Mississippi to spend time with tornado survivors. In every place, I met people whose lives were forever changed.

So much of the job of First Lady is to sit with people having the worst day of their life—wounded warriors, survivors of hurricanes, parents who've lost children to gun violence—to just *be* with them, to hold their hand and look in their eyes and tell them that they don't need to go through it alone. To me, that task was a great honor, and it required all my strength and composure. I had to be fully present. I had to keep any distractions, any of my own anxieties or sorrows, at bay so I could absorb theirs.

In June 2021, at a hotel ballroom where survivors of the Surfside,

Florida, building collapse had gathered, I spent hours going from table to table, visiting with almost a hundred grieving families—including a mother who was understandably inconsolable after losing her newlywed daughter and son-in-law, and two sons who lost both parents in their sixties.

When Maui suffered from catastrophic fires in 2023, we traveled to Hawaii for the day to survey the damage of the fires and grieve with the people of the state. As we were given an aerial tour of the destruction, I was rendered speechless. On the ground, surrounded by charred houses, cars, and trees, we met with families who cried and asked for help for their communities. We learned that 850 people were still missing, an impossible number of families whose hope was diminishing by the hour. Thousands were still without power. Everyone seemed stunned. The acrid odor that burned your nostrils, the flakes of ash on your clothing, the heat so hot it melted the tires—how could someone live through a fire like that and ever feel normal again?

To get through that day took all the strength I could muster. As always, I tried to focus on the victims and the people who were making things better and bringing hope to the situation—the rescue workers and local leaders working around the clock. Joe and I were astounded to find a 150-year-old banyan tree still alive in spite of its scorch marks. We took part in a ceremonial blessing involving bamboo stalks and palm fronds. As we flew away, I was reassured to know that a thousand federal officials were there leading response efforts, and that Joe had made sure the region received millions in aid to rebuild. Still, that horrible burning smell will always stay with me.

When tragedy strikes, it's amazing to see how people and organizations come together to help those in need. FEMA, headed by Deanne Criswell, was always one of the first response teams to arrive, followed by the Red Cross, National Guard, United Way, and International Association of Fire Fighters, to name just a few. José Andrés's World Central Kitchen appears wherever they're needed. Not to mention mental health care and animal rescue workers. We are so blessed to live in a country where the federal and state governments offer so much support. People helping people—the strength of who we are as Americans.

The question of whether to go in person to the site of a tragedy was always an easy one for me: You show up, the same way you mail a condolence card when someone you know dies and get a baby gift when someone has a shower. Politics, though, complicated even these basic human gestures.

In November 2021, an SUV plowed into a holiday parade in Waukesha, Wisconsin, and killed members of a longtime dance troupe called the Milwaukee Dancing Grannies. I said I was going to visit. Some of Joe's advisors said, "That's a red area. Don't go."

I couldn't bear not to go somewhere that had experienced that kind of tragedy just because few there had voted for Joe. We were president and First Lady for all Americans. I laid a wreath at the memorial and then went to city hall to meet with the victims' families. Out front, there were protesters, and the mood inside was tense. I went up to people and introduced myself. "Call me Jill," I said, over and over. Gradually, everyone relaxed. By the end, women were coming up to hug me and ask, "Can you take a picture with my daughter?"

In Lewiston, Maine, in November 2023 there had been a shooting at a bowling alley and a bar. We were there to honor the dead and to do what we could to comfort the survivors. Outside, protesters were screaming, cursing, holding up violent signs. Even though there was no credible evidence that Joe hadn't won the election, he was still being accused of stealing it. The country was already fractured by COVID and then the January 6 insurrection, and the surrounding conspiracy theories about the election made it much, much worse.

On another trip to Hawaii, which was a mostly blue state, I'd visited a school and was leaving to go back to the car when a protest descended. In the security field, they tend to especially worry about moving crowds, because those can get unruly. I was concerned they were going to trap us between buildings. But my aide and I moved swiftly. By the time we got back to the car, we were trembling.

I understood why I was often advised not to go to MAGA strongholds. But to me, finding ways to grieve together outweighed every other consideration. It's what makes us human. So I went to places where they hadn't voted for Joe because we'd promised to serve everyone, not just blue states. I offered my hand to whomever was in front of me, whether they shook it or not.

The philosopher Albert Camus wrote, "In the midst of winter, I found there was, within me, an invincible summer." Going around the country in the wake of tragedy, I tried to bring some message of hope into the dark places.

It never got easier visiting the sites of mass shootings. On January 8, 2011, nineteen people were shot in a Tucson parking lot as Congresswoman Gabby Giffords spoke to her constituents. After being shot in the head, Gabby persevered through a difficult recovery and became a strong advocate against gun violence. In the years that followed, I came to be in awe of Gabby. She'd seen the darkest parts of the human heart, and she'd responded by becoming a light to so many others. In June 2023, I spoke at the Giffords Law Center's thirtieth-anniversary celebration in San Francisco about the experience of bearing witness to so many gun deaths.

When I learned about thirteen-year-old shooting survivor Ava Olsen, from Townville, South Carolina, I thought, *Her friend Jacob will never grow up.* Ava would try out different clothing trends and learn to drive. She'd have crushes and graduate from high school. But Jacob, the boy she imagined marrying, now forever dressed in his favorite Batman costume, would always be six.

After years of debilitating PTSD, unable to leave her home for fear of loud noises that would force her to relive those moments on the playground when she ran for her life, Ava returned to her studies. But the heaviness of Jacob's small coffin would always weigh on her heart.

When I contemplated the state of gun laws in our country, I thought of those children who never got to grow up.

Daniel Barden of Newtown would always be seven.

Jaime Guttenberg of Parkland would always be fourteen.

Hallie Scruggs of Nashville would always be nine.

The number of children we've lost to mass shootings is unfathomable. The number of parents and siblings, teachers, journalists, police—innocent bystanders of every age. Those who died next to Gabby. Every massacre that turns our city names into synonyms for death.

The lives lost don't tell the whole story. They don't tell us of the loved ones who must live with a black hole of grief inside them, forever trapped in that gravity. They don't tell us of the classmates and coworkers who saw the blood, who heard the shots ring out, who wake each night in a sweat from nightmares where they're running and running.

Of the students who learn to live with fear, who know how to hide before they can spell.

The parents who must steel themselves as they put their children on the bus each morning. The congregants who watch the door instead of the pulpit. The communities of color who wonder when hate will shadow their doorstep with an AR-15 in hand. The places where gun violence is too common to make the nightly news.

As a teacher, I imagined the scene in my own classroom more times than I could count. At the start of each semester, I had to explain to my students what they should do if, God forbid, there was an active shooter. We all feel the ripple effects. We've all lost a piece of ourselves—our security, our hope, our trust in one another. If we supported the work of people like Gabby, we could build a future where we hear loud noises without ducking for cover. Where we shop for groceries and go to movies without fear. Where children like Daniel, Jaime, and Hallie would have been able to grow up.

When Joe and I visited the Uvalde memorial—just twelve days after we mourned with people who'd lost friends and relatives in a Buffalo, New York, grocery store shooting—we stood in front of twenty-one crosses. I touched the pictures of the bright, beautiful faces of children who would never again laugh or open birthday presents or tell their parents that they loved them. Teachers fell into my arms crying. We went to Mass at Sacred Heart with families broken by grief. As we were leaving the sanctuary, someone in the crowd, articulating the desperation so many of us felt, yelled, "Do something!"

Joe worked with Congress to pass the first major gun safety law in almost thirty years. Because of him, there was a mechanism in place to stop domestic abusers from buying guns. We strengthened background checks for young people. We increased funding for mental health programs and school security. Joe took dozens of executive actions to keep firearms out of the hands of dangerous people and save lives.

Gabby Giffords came out in the wake of the 2024 election with words of comfort once again: "After being shot in the head and nearly killed, it would have been easy to lose hope—but I never did. Despite all the pain, I held on to my hopes for this country every bit as tightly as I did the hope that I would one day take a walk or talk with my family. I learned that trying times bring out the power of the human spirit."

When Joe and I moved into the White House in January 2021, it felt as though we had the wind at our back. There was hope and promise. We could all breathe a bit more easily. Then, within months, the wind shifted.

CHAPTER 16

Joe fulfilled a campaign promise and ended the forever war in Afghanistan—a move most Americans supported. He knew it was always going to be difficult to extricate American troops while maintaining a stable government, but the end on August 30, 2021, was something no one could have predicted.

We had spent a lot of time at Walter Reed National Military Medical Center, at the bedside of wounded warriors. When Joe was vice president, we'd gone almost every Christmas as the wars raged on. I'd go from room to room to room, spending hours talking to people while taking in their cross-stitched bodies and red-raw skin set against the starched white sheets. I'd always been anti-war, but seeing the suffering of those men and women had made it obvious to me that putting our troops in combat should always be a last resort.

Many of those who came home wounded were young, and I met countless parents who had to take care of them for the rest of their lives. One parent would be working. The other would be taking care of the former service member—giving them their medications, combing their hair, helping them get out of bed, protecting them from loud noises or crowds or other things that made their mental health struggles worse. As long as wars were being fought, their ranks were growing, and they were largely forgotten. The debt we owe our military and their families became even more visible to me in 2008 when Beau was in Iraq.

When Beau came home, I asked him, "What do the soldiers need most after fighting in war?"

"Mental health, Mom," he said.

When I traveled to military bases, I saw how increasing access to telehealth helped take away the stigma of those suffering from PTSD or brain trauma. At Walter Reed, I saw how art therapy let service members express their anxiety and challenges in creative ways.

Then there were the children—thousands of them who took care of an injured parent while the other parent worked. They would administer medicines, help them exercise, feed them, do whatever was needed that day. These children were true heroes.

When Gabby Rodriguez was little, she used to ask other five- and six-year-olds on the playground, "Was your dad in the military? Does he have a boo-boo on his brain?" At age nine, she helped her mom take care of her injured father. Zianny Pabon, age twelve, helped her dad keep track of his medications and doctor appointments. Noah Stephens, age twenty, had learned how to help his dad through a seizure if his mother wasn't home. Mason Wilson, just six years old, had become the family entertainer, always ready with a joke or story to put a smile on his parents' faces when things seemed hopeless.

We partnered with the Elizabeth Dole Foundation to launch the Hidden Helpers Coalition, a national alliance made up of public and private sector organizations seeking to uplift the voices of military and veteran caregiver children.

As the promised withdrawal from Afghanistan approached, Joe's military advisors seemed to be fiercely divided about how best to get out. I watched on television, like everyone else, as the pullout took place. Intelligence did not seem to anticipate how fast the Taliban would take over once we left, and how hard it would be to get our allies out of harm's way. On August 26, an ISIS suicide bombing at the Kabul airport killed thirteen members of our military along with 170 Afghans.

I will always hold the memory of the fallen American service members in my heart: Marine Corps Lance Cpl. David L. Espinoza, Marine Corps Sgt. Nicole L. Gee, Marine Corps Staff Sgt. Darin T. Hoover, Army Staff Sgt. Ryan C. Knauss, Marine Corps Cpl. Hunter Lopez, Marine Corps Lance Cpl. Rylee J. McCollum, Marine Corps Lance Cpl. Dylan R. Merola, Marine Corps Lance Cpl. Kareem M. Nikoui, Marine Corps Cpl. Daegan W. Page, Marine Corps Sgt. Johanny Rosario Pichardo, Marine Corps Cpl. Humberto A. Sanchez, Marine Corps Lance Cpl. Jared M. Schmitz, and Navy Hospital Corpsman Maxton W. Soviak.

Joe took full responsibility, and yet that would mark the first time we went into a group of military families and were met not as friends but, by some, as enemies. Joe called each family to offer condolences and listen to them. Then we traveled to meet with them in person and to oversee what's called the "dignified transfer," or ceremonial return, of the fallen at Dover Air Force Base.

Dover Air Force Base in Delaware is where dignified transfers take place for all branches of the military. The work they do is difficult, and they carry out their work with such deep respect. I had been there before for a dignified transfer when I was Second Lady. In the past, families were held in a rather cold room. Then the military recognized that it needed a comfortable space. They built the Families of the Fallen Center in 2009–2010 at the height of the wars on terror.

The mortuary on the base receives the warrior, and there are closely followed protocols intended to treat every man and woman with the utmost respect and dignity. The families usually arrive the day before the transfer and receive a steady flow of clergy, military officials, and representatives of the government. After arriving early that morning, Joe and I were given a thorough briefing by the military. We knew the exact minute each movement would take place, were told precisely where to stand and when to salute. From there, we were taken to the center to meet the families.

We slowly walked in. The families—all thirteen—were gathered in one large, open, dimly lit room filled with soft living room furniture and table lamps. I took a deep breath and steeled myself. I had to be strong for them. Some were vocal. Some turned their backs. Most were weeping. It had been three days or less since the families had gotten the news about their child's or their spouse's death. Flown from all over the United States, and taken to the Fisher House on the base, they were still in shock. It was too much for them to absorb. There was no privacy for anyone. Then they had to come face-to-face with the man who had taken responsibility for their loved one's death. We were there to hold them when they'd let us, do whatever we could to show that we understood their pain. We'd lost a child. Joe had lost two. There was still nothing we could do to remove their sorrow. Not then, not ever. Then we proceeded to the flight line.

Breathe, I told myself.

We stood directly across from the families with Secretary of State Antony Blinken, Secretary of Defense Lloyd Austin, and the chairman of the Joint Chiefs of Staff, Mark Milley.

I could hear crying, but I couldn't look at the families for fear of losing my composure. I knew their pain was excruciating. Seeing the flag-draped coffins made it real.

Breathe.

One by one, each service member was transferred on their way "home."

Sergeant Nicole Gee had deployed from Camp Lejeune in North Carolina. I had been to Lejeune a few times and I wanted to visit to offer my condolences and spend more time with those grieving. They'd set out the powerful marker of lost service members, empty boots in a row. Where Sergeant Gee had left her car parked before leaving for Afghanistan, a makeshift memorial appeared. I placed a bouquet of roses on the windshield and said a prayer for her.

I was supposed to meet with Nicole's best friend, but she'd tested positive for COVID. I learned that she was sitting in her car nearby, so I went over and placed a white rose on her windshield and put my hand on it. Her hand touched mine through the glass as she wept, enveloped in sorrow.

"I'm so sorry," I said, loud enough so she could hear me through the glass. "I'll be in touch. God bless you."

I called the next day to tell her I was thinking of her, and we kept in touch.

I knew that in the wake of the Iraq War, in which 4,432 US service members lost their lives and close to 32,000 were wounded, President George W. Bush encountered parents who blamed him for the death of their children. Joe and I hadn't experienced that until the withdrawal from Afghanistan, but at that dignified transfer, a number of those thirteen grieving families expressed their pain.

The tragedy in Afghanistan was a turning point for Joe's administration. We'd started the year carried by the country's high hopes and expectations. By so many across the country, Joe was beloved, hailed as a savior. His COVID strategy was working. People were able to gather again safely. The economy was coming back to life. The divisions of the former administration seemed to be healing. But that summer changed everything.

I sometimes wrote Joe notes in lipstick on the mirror in his bathroom, where I knew he'd see them as he shaved. Sometimes just a heart. Other times, "You're my hero." On my way to work one morning, seeing how much negativity Joe was facing, I left him a note that said, "Get up, champ. Get up"—something his father always said to him in hard times.

CHAPTER 17

When I read the *New York Times* article "Study Shows the Staggering Cost of Menopause for Women in the Work Force," I was struck by how much women have suffered unnecessarily, whether in menopause or pregnancy or at any other stage of life. The article said that our country loses $1.8 billion in working time every year to the menopause symptoms that upend women's lives. It struck me that I'd experienced those kinds of symptoms, too, as had many of my friends, but I'd thought, *That's just the way life is, isn't it?*

For decades—for centuries, even—at dinner tables and in waiting rooms, in whispered conversations around the water cooler, women have been talking to each other about our health, searching for answers. How many women did I know who'd gone to a doctor with debilitating pain and been told "It's all in your head" or "It's just stress"? More than I could count.

It was an ordinary Saturday in late April 2023 when I read that *Times* story. That afternoon, I was in my office in the East Wing doing what community college teachers do on weekends, especially late in the semester: grading papers. Maria Shriver, the former First Lady of California, came in for a meeting. We began discussing the article, and she told me that it's not just menopause symptoms that don't have enough treatment options. It's all of women's health—for our whole bodies, for our whole lives.

It's a problem that's so easy to see, yet often ignored. Women's health is understudied and research is underfunded. Until the mid-1990s, women were not required to be included in federally funded research—and they often weren't. From 2013 to 2023, only 8.8 percent of National Institutes of Health (NIH) research grant spending went toward women's health research. As a result, too many of our medications, treatments, health products, and medical school textbooks have been based on men.

This has created gaps in our understanding of conditions that mostly affect women, only affect women, or affect women and men differently, leaving women seeking health care in a medical world largely designed for men's bodies. Improving women's health requires understanding those conditions. The discoveries we could make would give us insight into all of human biology.

It was one of those moments that happen in life, where you learn something and you can never see the world the same way again. Suddenly, the problem felt so familiar—because we all know what Maria was talking about. If you ask any woman in America about her health care, she probably has a story to tell. You know her.

She's the woman who gets debilitating migraines but doesn't know why, and can't find treatment options that work for her.

She's the woman going through menopause, who visits her doctor and leaves with more questions than answers, even though half the country will go through menopause at some point in their lives.

She's the woman whose heart attack isn't recognized because her symptoms don't look like a man's, even as heart disease is the leading cause of death among women.

She's the woman who needs treatments, and affordable and easy-to-use products that help her stay healthy or feel better when health needs arise.

That same night, I asked Joe at dinner what he thought could be done. He never wasted time to act when a problem was identified. In a few short months, we launched the first-ever White House Initiative on Women's Health Research. Through this effort, we set out to fundamentally change how the United States approaches and funds research on women's health.

In March 2024, Joe signed the Executive Order on Advancing Women's Health Research and Innovation to ensure federal agencies strengthened their research and data standards to enhance the study of women's health across federally funded research.

As a result, for example, the Congressionally Directed Medical Research Programs, run by the Department of Defense (DOD), implemented a policy to ensure researchers use both male and female study subjects unless there's a good reason not to do so. His executive order directed agencies to prioritize grantmaking to researchers and entrepreneurs focused on women's health, including through the Advanced Research Projects Agency for Health (ARPA-H) and the NIH.

It also directed the US secretary of Health and Human Services to address research gaps related to menopause and women's midlife health, the secretaries of Defense and Veterans Affairs to support the needs of women service members and veterans related to midlife health, and the director of the National Science Foundation to consider how artificial intelligence might be used to the benefit of women's health research.

Thanks to the executive order, our White House Initiative galvanized nearly $1 billion in funding for women's health research, through agencies like the NIH, DOD, and ARPA-H. These investments aimed to advance research to improve prevention, diagnosis, and treatment of diseases and conditions that affect women uniquely, differently, and disproportionately—from menopause to brain disorders to cardiovascular disease. In his State of the Union, Joe called on Congress to provide $12 billion for women's health research, to help make up for all the lost time. While Congress didn't get that done, I hope a future administration will deliver this needed funding.

ARPA-H is a legacy of Joe's administration that few people talk about but that will have a massive impact on the health of Americans. Modeled on the Defense Advanced Research Projects Agency (DARPA), the defense agency that helped bring us once-unimaginable technologies like the internet, satellites, flat-screens, and Siri, ARPA-H pursues the kind of breakthroughs in health that could change everything. Joe created this agency because he knew we needed faster and better cures—as anyone who has lost a family member to a terrible disease like cancer knows.

When we began our initiative, ARPA-H was one of the first places Joe turned. Led by the remarkable Dr. Renee Wegrzyn, the agency launched the Sprint for Women's Health program, investing $113 million in researchers and entrepreneurs working on solutions like noninvasive blood tests for endometriosis, new ovarian treatments to prevent disease in menopause, and a first-of-its-kind at-home test for the early detection of preeclampsia. These scientists and entrepreneurs should give us all such great hope.

My visits to research labs have opened my eyes to how many brilliant scientists we have working in this country. One scientist I encountered had isolated the gene that causes some women to have severe nausea during pregnancy. She found that a hormone produced by the fetus could trigger morning sickness in women who were particularly sensitive to it. Hearing about the doctor's work made me feel like I was watching the Tuesday Science section of *The New York Times* (my favorite read of the week) come to life.

How proud I was that the boom in research and innovation that Joe fostered would result in greater health and wellness for American women, the discovery of new treatments for disease, and new ways for us to live longer and stay stronger. I spoke at forums on women's health alongside some of our greatest doctors—and celebrities boldly admitting that they, too, struggled with the physical challenges of midlife.

As my husband said at our White House Conference on Women's Health Research in December 2024, "The work we're doing on women's health research is some of the most important work this administration has ever done."

I'm biased, but seeing all the momentum in the field today, I agree!

"Well, Jill, then you shouldn't go to college."

That's what my high school guidance counselor told me.

I was crushed. His assessment was that I wasn't college material.

He said, "If you don't really know what you want to do next, college just isn't right for you. You shouldn't waste your time."

My whole life, I'd wanted to go to college. And now the person who was supposed to guide me there was saying I couldn't do it.

Well, I got my college degree—and, at the age of fifty-five, I walked across that graduation stage to receive my doctorate.

People like to tell us what they think we can't do, don't they? They say it's going to be too hard or too complicated. That no one like you has done this before.

In my advocacy for community colleges, I was determined to make attending them free for students who qualified. This was an effort I started as Second Lady through the College Promise initiative. This work resulted in thirty-five state-led efforts to make community college free. When Joe was elected, I wanted this opportunity to be available for all students in all communities. My policy team worked to add free community college to a bill that was moving through Congress in spring 2021. These weren't just associate degrees, either—workforce development programs were also partnering with community colleges. Students could sign up for certificate programs that ended with them being given a good trade job in, say, carpentry or electrical work, all debt-free.

As a teacher, I'd seen firsthand how community college supported students educationally, vocationally, and personally. I'd also seen how even the low cost of tuition at these schools could be prohibitive for worthy students who wanted to attend.

Senator Mitch McConnell made passing Joe's bipartisan Investment and Jobs Act all but impossible, though pieces of it looked as though they might survive. Free community college had support from both sides of the aisle and a real chance of passing—except there were two key votes against it: Arizona Senator Kyrsten Sinema and West Virginia Senator Joe Manchin.

I went to West Virginia for a vaccine-promotion trip with Jennifer Garner, who I'd served with on the board of Save the Children—she grew up in Charleston, West Virginia, and her mom still lives there. We invited Senator Manchin and his wife, Gayle, to join us. I took the opportunity to mention that I thought means-tested free community college could make a huge difference to people like my students trying to get an education even against steep odds.

Manchin told me that churches should take care of helping families in need, and that it was his experience that paying for college yourself helps you learn to value it. He said he knew people who'd failed out when it was being paid for by other people and who'd really appreciated it when they had to foot the bill themselves.

Another time, I lobbied Manchin after a meeting he had with Joe at the White House, telling him my students' stories, hoping to move him with how much good increasing access for them could do. I talked about how many more women were getting into building trades and becoming electricians and carpenters. I'd gotten to know many of the country's community college presidents, and I offered to put him in touch with them.

He listened, but in the end, the money was going to go to funding either community college or early childhood education. I didn't want to compete against pre-K. I believe above all else that early childhood education is essential for student success.

I was scheduled to meet Joe's policy team and senior staff in the Roosevelt Room to discuss the bill. I received a heads-up that they were going to ask me to pull back on free community college so that the bill could move forward. So I put on a dark blue suit and a black armband. It was my own personal protest. When I walked in the room and they saw what I was wearing, we all broke out into laughter. But I did want to make a point.

Losses like that made the victories even more meaningful.

Like a spell, the word "cancer" stills the air around us—frozen in place, we feel the world as we knew it slipping away. In the span of a breath, a thousand questions fill our minds: *What can I do? How do I tell people? Why did this happen?* And when the hands of the clock begin to move once again, we are not the person we once were, but someone changed.

Cancer touches everyone.

One of our successes was establishing insurance coverage for patient navigators.

Having navigated the medical system following family cancer diagnoses, I know well that when you hear the news, you're so shell-shocked that you don't know what to do, what your next step is. Typically you get out your phone and start googling—and scare the hell out of yourself. Patient navigation was a solution, and I made advocacy for it a priority when we relaunched the Cancer Moonshot during Joe's presidency.

In November 2023, the Biden administration announced that Medicare would pay for navigation services. The administration also announced medical billing codes that enable private health insurers to pay for these services as well. This advanced a new era in cancer treatment.

When my class's writing tutor, Paula, found out she had lymphoma, she was devastated. It made things just a little bit easier when, with the help of an assigned guide, she was able to figure out a treatment plan that worked for her. Newly optimistic about her future, she emailed me to say, "My patient navigator just called me, and I thought of you."

I am proud of my team for working so quickly to make patient navigation a reality for American families.

CHAPTER 18

You cannot go into a war zone and come away unchanged. You don't have to see the sorrow with your eyes because you can feel it with your heart. The thing about grief is that it veils one's face. It's like a haze has descended. The tears of mothers stay permanently on the edges of their eyes, as if they can hardly contain their sadness. They grasp their children's hands or touch their hair, as if they can't bear to lose the physical connection. Their emotion is visible in the slope of their shoulders, the nervousness in their bodies. Something is missing—laughter, a common language among women.

On February 24, 2022, Vladimir Putin launched a full-scale attack on Ukraine. It was all so senseless and heartbreaking. I felt that I had to do something to show America's solidarity with the Ukrainian people. So many of them had served alongside our men and women post-9/11, as I had learned when I traveled to Iraq to visit our service members stationed there.

In the weeks after the Ukraine invasion, I spoke with Poland's First Lady, Agata Kornhauser-Duda. She briefed me on what they were experiencing in Poland. I asked how I could best express my concern for Ukraine and support the border countries absorbing refugees. I discussed those possibilities with my team and tasked them with quietly investigating what a trip to the region might look like. How would we get there safely? What would be required? Was it even possible?

The official press release we issued before my trip read:

> The First Lady will spend Mother's Day weekend traveling to Romania and Slovakia to visit with US troops, reaffirm our strong bilateral ties with these two NATO allies, hear from Ukrainian refugees, show support for the Ukrainian people, and express gratitude for the relief efforts of neighboring countries, United Nations (UN) agencies, and nongovernmental organizations (NGOs). Dr. Biden is inspired by the resilience and strength of the Ukrainian people and hopes to communicate that Americans are standing with them. On Mother's Day, she will meet with Ukrainian mothers and children who have been forced to flee their home country because of Putin's war.

On Sunday, May 8, we flew to Košice, Slovakia, where we saw a city-run refugee center and a school. Next, we traveled to the Slovakia-Ukraine border crossing in Vyšné Nemecké, Slovakia, where Ukrainian refugees could enter Slovakia and receive basic services before moving on to processing centers or transit hubs further inside the country.

Border guards told me stories of thousands of people who crossed into Slovakia fleeing Russia's unjust invasion. In the cold of February, many walked for miles upon miles with no shoes. They were fleeing in fear, hoping to find safety and then one day return home. One eleven-year-old traveled by himself, with only a phone number to contact his family written on his arm. Others even had pets making the journey with them. "We weren't ready for that," the guards told me. We had seen images of these crossings for months, but hearing the stories directly was chilling.

Our final preannounced stop was to visit a facility provided by the local Greek Catholic church that served refugees, volunteers, NGO workers, and first responders. As we left the church, though, we didn't proceed back to our original motorcade. We were met by a second, new motorcade of armored vehicles. From there we quickly drove into Ukraine. This part of the itinerary had been tightly choreographed, but it was kept a surprise for safety reasons. Only once we were out of the country would the press be able to report on this portion of the trip.

It was eerily quiet as we drove through Ukraine. We were at times the only car on the road, driving through miles and miles of bright yellow sunflower fields that almost seemed to be glowing in contrast with the blue sky.

My car pulled up to the austere building in the city of Uzhhorod at the same time another car arrived. We opened the doors, and Ukraine's First Lady Olena Zelenska and I both got out and hugged. I handed her flowers, and we whispered "Happy Mother's Day" to each other. I told her I was in Ukraine carrying the hearts of the American people with me.

"Thank you," Zelenska responded. "The Ukrainians are so grateful for the support of the American people."

We went into the makeshift shelter built in a former school. People were sleeping on the floor. The gymnasium was packed full of mothers, children, and pets, all of whom seemed to be in shock. Olena and I talked to Ukrainian women who told us about trying to get food for their children. The men weren't there; they were away fighting. The mothers had tables set up for children to do crafts, to try to keep them busy and give them some sense of normality. The women gently encouraged their children to sing, to color pictures, to stay calm—even while they themselves were scared to death.

The Ukrainian mothers I visited told me about the horrors of the bombs that fell night after night as they sought to find refuge during their journey westward. Many had to live days without food and sunlight, harbored in basements. The scale of the suffering was hard to fathom.

One young Ukrainian mother I met told me that when she and her family ventured out in search of food, Russian soldiers would shoot into the lines of people waiting for a piece of bread. These women were grateful to the people of Romania and Slovakia for their support. As another mother, Anna, told me, "There are no borders for our hearts."

Although Olena Zelenska seemed comfortable in my presence, she rarely looked me in the eye when speaking to me, which she did in English. Clad in a blazer, jeans, and white sneakers, she wrapped her arms around her body unconsciously. She seemed to be on high alert at all times, ready for anything to happen.

Olena told me of widespread rape, and about the many children who had seen people shot and killed, their homes burned. She didn't ask me for food or clothing or weapons. What she requested was help supplying mental health care to those suffering from the effects of Vladimir Putin's brutality.

To visit with me, Olena had come out of hiding. As we finished our meeting and gave each other one last hug, she quietly told me, "I want to return home quickly. I only want to hold the hands of my children."

Kahlil Gibran wrote, "The deeper that sorrow carves into your being, the more joy you can contain." My hope is that this is true for the mothers I met. But that can only happen when this war ends. On the flight to Washington, I wrote an op-ed for CNN that ended: "Mr. Putin, please end this senseless and brutal war." That plea has gone unanswered.

CHAPTER 19

We were spending a rare weekend at the White House rather than in Delaware. Prior to Joe serving as vice president, we had never lived in Washington, so we took advantage of the proximity to our home and spent most weekends there, where we could be close to family. But this weekend, we were in DC because Joe was being interviewed by Special Counsel Robert Hur regarding classified documents.

The issue arose when Joe's West Wing office was packed up at the end of the Obama administration. A harried aide had packed a dozen boxes without noticing that there were classified documents in among the personal letters, speeches, and photographs. Hur would come to decide that no criminal charges against Joe were warranted.

Then, very early on the morning of Saturday, October 7, 2023, I was grading midterms when the staff texted me and asked if Joe was up yet—he had to get on the phone with the National Security Council. I turned on the news and saw what was happening. Hamas had viciously killed, raped, and burned innocent Israeli civilians.

That week was filled with sadness and mourning. Israeli Prime Minister Benjamin Netanyahu responded to the terrorist attack by declaring, "We are at war." No one quite knew what that would mean at the time—how many people would die, how many countries would become embroiled—but we knew Netanyahu would seek to remove Hamas from power to keep Israel safe.

America's support for Israel was clear. There was outrage and condemnation of the attack. Joe wanted to stand with the people of Israel. He flew to meet Netanyahu in solidarity. But weeks turned into months. The Palestinian death toll rose. The images of starving children and cities turned to rubble were causing people of conscience around the world to ask when it would ever stop.

Pope Francis reached out to Joe to discuss the war, especially the release of hostages and the importance of protecting civilians. During the call, Joe asked the pope to pray for him. Francis asked Joe to pray for him, too. This was not the first time they'd spoken—they'd met in person several times, including two years earlier—but it might have been the most powerful of their conversations. Francis kept repeating to Joe: "You are a man of peace."

As Second Lady, I'd borne witness to drought and famine, as at the Dadaab refugee camp in Kenya, and I'd visited crisis regions as the board chair of Save the Children from 2017 to 2019. I'd been impressed by the relief work of the great chef and humanitarian José Andrés, who in 2010 started World Central Kitchen, getting food to where it was needed most. He has said, "The dishes we cook and deliver are not just ingredients, or calories. A plate of food is a plate of hope. A message that someone, somewhere, cares for you."

Again, I feel that we need to look for and celebrate those who bring aid and care into situations that feel dire and hopeless. José Andrés is such a man.

On April 2, 2024, before going to teach, I was putting on makeup with the morning news on in the background when I heard that seven of José's aid workers on a mission of peace were killed by Israeli bombs. I felt devastated.

For weeks, I had been begging Joe to do anything he could to pursue a ceasefire in the Israel-Hamas war. Of course I was aware that there was so much I didn't know. Much of what Joe was seeing was classified. But when Israeli forces killed the World Central Kitchen workers, I felt like I had to say something. I usually woke up before Joe, so I saw before he did the horrors he'd have to confront. That morning, seeing yet another day of devastation in Gaza, I left a Post-it note for Joe on the mirror above his sink before I left to teach so he would see it when he got up: "WCK aid workers killed (1 Amer). Net has to stop."

Well, this was a private note between us, but at a meeting that morning, Joe read it out loud. I was on my lunch break at NOVA when I got a call saying that a Katie Rogers story about my note would be appearing in *The New York Times*. My aides wanted to know: Was this true? What exactly did I say? I was initially angry at the aides, thinking they were chastising me. What a lesson in the price of speaking up! Ten words on a Post-it urging peace and I was in trouble? My press secretary said no, she just needed to know what to say to Rogers about it.

Yes, I had written it, I told them. The article came out with the headline, "'Stop It Now': Jill Biden Privately Urges an End to Conflict in Gaza." The next morning, I left another note knowing Joe was going to be talking to Netanyahu: "Be strong. Don't let BN use your goodness."

That time I added that he should please keep the note between us.

CHAPTER 20

We hosted several hundred events a year at the White House, everything from a small military retirement party or a Make-A-Wish child visit to state dinners for hundreds of people in formal dress.

Regardless of the size of the group, photos and handshakes were part of the schedule. At larger events, the photo lines were typically three hundred people plus. I developed terrible wrist pain from shaking so many hands a day. There were times when to keep going I'd have to run upstairs and plunge my hand into a bucket of ice (a trick Hillary Clinton taught me). We tried to move things along quickly, but Joe, as I've said before, wanted to talk to everyone for hours. He'd grown immune over the years to my *let's move it along* throat-clearing and arm-squeeze signals. Social aides often had to swoop in to encourage lingering guests with a friendly "This way, sir . . ." Thank God for the social aides.

Of course, there is nothing more elegant than a state dinner. The White House staff outdoes itself to make everything beautiful, and the presence of world leaders and celebrities creates a buzz of excitement. As First Lady, you must make dozens of choices—every color, every flower, every course. Everything is scripted down to the minute, and every decision is sure to be dissected both by guests and by the press. I was so fortunate to have Carlos Elizondo, the White House social secretary, as my partner. We had worked together for eight years when Joe was vice president. I told Carlos that if Joe were ever elected president, he would be my first call. And he was.

Inevitably, someone still complains about something being too this or too that. Some people are mad that they can't bring their whole families. Others arrive in the room and decide that their table doesn't have enough star power, then have the audacity to switch place cards or to put in elaborate requests: "I don't want so-and-so in my line of sight." The power plays amaze me, as does the extent to which visitors covet anything with the presidential seal on it. They often tuck a few extra White House paper towels into their purse as a remembrance. God forbid you're the last one in the ladies' room—there are often none left to dry your hands!

Something always required reshuffling. At the India state dinner in June 2023, we thought we'd be safe with a vegetarian menu, but there were dozens of last-minute requests for vegan, dairy-free, and garlic-free meals. The kitchen had its hands full adjusting plates to meet the guests' needs. We found out last minute that the chandeliers we'd rented for the Australian dinner in October 2023 were too heavy for the tents we'd planned to hang them in, and we wound up having to arrange for new lighting.

At one state dinner, the visitors from Africa hadn't been given enough time to overcome jet lag, so they were falling asleep at the table. I asked the staff to speed the courses along as quickly as possible so that the guests could finish their meals and go straight to bed.

The first state dinner I hosted, for France, in December 2022, was so effervescent, it felt as though we could have kept the party going until dawn. The decor was red, white, and blue, for our shared national colors. The guest list was a mix of dignitaries and cultural figures. I invited Tara Westover, the author of *Educated*, and sat her and her boyfriend at my table. Emmanuel Macron sat to my right. He was a great dinner partner—chatty and interesting—and kept the conversation going. The brilliant Jon Batiste performed, and brought the house down with one of my favorite of his songs, "Cry." His whole family came, and they had everyone dancing in the aisles.

I'd done countless tastings to arrive at the menu. It was important to me that the food not be messy to eat. I thought of the woman who buys a beautiful dress and winds up with sauce all over it. Forget about leafy frisée salads covered in dressing. You had to be able to get it in your mouth in one bite. I also had to make sure the wines paired well, which often meant trying a flight of wines alongside the food samples at ten in the morning. We wound up serving butter-poached Maine lobster and coulotte of beef. I went back and forth on whether to serve a pre-dessert cheese plate per French tradition. In the end, I did that, only with American cheeses. The French seemed to enjoy those more than the California wines.

When it came to picking my outfit, Bailey Moon was my stylist, and my trusted longtime aide Jordan Montoya kept me true to myself. We worked with designers to find something culturally appropriate—so, no white if the country we're hosting is India, China, or Japan, as white symbolizes death in those cultures. Sometimes I was told by the State Department that I should wear something specific for a particular cultural event. For the French dinner, I wore a navy off-the-shoulder Oscar de la Renta gown designed by Laura Kim and Fernando Garcia.

You really never knew what would happen at a state dinner, in spite of all the formality and preparation. In April 2023, the South Korean president wound up coming onstage to sing—impeccably—one of his favorite songs, “American Pie.”

In May 2024, I hosted the first-ever Teachers of the Year state dinner, and I loved every minute of it. Fifty-five teachers attended, with representatives from each state and territory. As a teacher of forty years, I feel a strong connection to all the educators I meet. We talk the same language. We know the challenges, but we're teachers because of the joys.

The centerpieces were book-themed. Golden apples were scattered on the tables. The vases were made from pencils. The featured flower was the iris, the Tennessee state flower—a nod to the National Teacher of the Year, Missy Testerman, an ESL specialist at Rogersville City School in a rural Appalachian community. We surprised the teachers with handwritten notes from their students, colleagues, and administrators. Another surprise was an appearance from Joe, who told the educators that they were the kite strings keeping our national ambitions aloft.

At the dinner, I announced our administration's efforts to improve teacher pay and enable Public Service Loan Forgiveness. I gave each teacher being celebrated a brass bell.

In my remarks, I explained:

“When I was a little girl, my grandmother would sometimes take me to school with her, a one-room schoolhouse in a small town in South Jersey. She loved her work, and her students loved her in return. And she used to call her students to class with a big brass bell. When she died, she didn't leave behind a giant estate. But what I inherited from her—what I still have to this day—is that bell. And I sometimes think about the way her legacy resonated into the world like waves of sound, changing those who heard its ring . . . Today, all of you ring your own bell—pulling each person you teach into a harmony that never ends."

I could hardly contain my excitement when I knew the strolling military chorus and strings were about to enter the room.

"Take out your phones!" I told the teachers. "Something's about to happen that you won't want to miss!" They filmed and cheered as the musicians wove in and out among the tables playing "Brave" and "Ain't No Mountain High Enough."

A first course of apple, walnut, and celery root salad was served, then lobster ravioli as a main course. To finish, White House executive pastry chef Susie Morrison made a dessert trio of coconut custard cake, apple mousse, and strawberries with cream. I'll never forget that night; it was pure joy. I'd never felt prouder to be an educator.

Our November 2024 dinner was held as a farewell to thank four hundred of the supporters who'd made Joe's term possible. We hadn't been able to fete them at the inauguration because of the pandemic.

The brilliant event planner Bryan Rafanelli created something truly incredible, putting up a clear-topped tent around the South Lawn fountain, enclosing it, and filling the space with globes of light and setting masses of pink roses standing up all the way around the fountain. The Secret Service initially blocked lines of sight as a precaution, but we worked with them to open up the back wall so that diners could see the monuments. It was magnificent.

In my toast to Joe, I said, "It's hard to believe that we're in the final moments of this extraordinary journey together . . . Joe, throughout your life in public service, you've put people at the center. So it's never a surprise to see people gather around you. Four years ago, you set out to restore the soul of the nation. It was never just a sound bite; it was your drumbeat. Your wisdom and steady hand lifted our country out of a pandemic, set our economy on solid ground, and fortified our hope for what is possible. You led with an unshakable belief in the goodness of the American people and guided us on a new and brighter course. All the while, you continued to be a brother, an uncle, a friend, a partner, and a father and grandfather whose devotion can be measured by the calls that you fit between bilateral meetings and security briefings—just to check in and say 'I love you.' What I've watched you do for more than forty years is extraordinary. What you've done over the last four years is breathtaking." I handed him a flute of ginger ale. "Please join me in raising a glass to your president—my husband and hero—Joe Biden."

With Joe at the helm, the country was a kinder place. In an atmosphere of compromise and compassion, I saw the nation healing. When I look back on my years at the White House, working in rooms that no longer exist, I see them as if inside a snow globe—this magical place filled with people trying to keep traditions alive. For posterity, it feels important to describe what life in the White House was like, before things changed.

CHAPTER 21

In 2021, to find a way to celebrate the holidays in spite of COVID, Trisha Yearwood and I taped a Food Network special called *White House Thanksgiving*, where we cooked a Thanksgiving meal together using recipes of hers and mine. We used vegetables and herbs from the kitchen garden, flowers from my cutting garden, and honey from the beehives. The White House kitchen was under construction, so we used Blair House's kitchen. Joking around in our White House aprons, Trisha said her husband, Garth Brooks, was a good cook. I couldn't say the same. "You do not want to eat anything Joe's cooked," I told her.

As we made the brine, trussed the turkey, and prepared the sides, we laughed a lot. Trisha said that in agreeing to disagree about whether the side dish was called dressing or stuffing, we were focusing on what united us, not what divided us. We prepared my Grandmom Jacobs's stuffing, which she always made using stale Italian bread. Trisha's grandmother used saltines, so we added some of those, too.

The White House executive chef Cristeta Comerford came by to give us advice on roasting the turkey (she crisps it up at 450° before lowering it to 350° for the rest of the cook time). Susie Morrison dropped by to help us make apple crisp with chocolate chip ice cream for Joe. I wrote everyone's names on their dessert plates in chocolate syrup and put the plates in the freezer. We served dinner in the Green Room, with candles and floral arrangements by Hedieh Ghaffarian on mix-and-match presidential china. Trisha said grace and then became emotional: "I just said my dad's prayer in the White House."

"Let's set the table Nana-style," my grandkids say when they're helping out with meals. That really touches my heart. Before holiday meals, we forage together for dried hydrangeas or anything else that we can find, and we arrange them into bouquets as decoration. The kids have always seemed to enjoy doing that with me. I hope those traditions will stick as they grow older and have their own families. When I hosted family parties at the White House, I tried to make the gatherings feel the same way, with lots of food and plenty of flowers and candles.

For Ashley's fortieth birthday in June 2021, I wanted to do something special. Ashley, a social worker with an MSW degree, has devoted her life to public service. A few years ago, she founded a women's wellness space in North Philadelphia for women who have been incarcerated. At the space, they're able to access education, health care, and mental health care. Ashley does everything from run yoga classes to assist women in applying for jobs. I've seen how hard it can be to carve out your own life when your parents are in the spotlight, but she's always been all about helping people, women in particular. She wears her heart on her sleeve. As the youngest child, she was definitely spoiled a bit by her dad, but now I see her spoiling him right back—popping over to have dinner with him just to cheer him up, taking him to medical appointments, and nudging him about his diet.

Joe and me in The Beast on our way to Arlington National Cemetery on Inauguration Day. January 2021.

Joe stopped by to say hello after I gave my convention speech from the Brandywine High School classroom where I taught in the early 1990s. Wilmington, Delaware, August 2020.

"Honk if you want America to be united again!" October 2020.

Campaigning during COVID, we had to get creative. I wore a lot of VOTE masks. October 2020.

Joe and I entered the White House via the Grand Foyer as the United States Marine Band played to welcome us on Inauguration Day.

I tried to make my East Wing office welcoming. Willow liked it, though I think her favorite place was the cat bed the residence staff kept for her upstairs.

Talented interior decorator Mark D. Sikes beautifully transformed my East Wing office.

I was grateful every day for my incredible staff, pictured here at Camp David. January 2024.

I've always hated needles, so I understood when people wanted a hand to hold at the countless COVID-19 vaccine clinics I visited that first year of Joe's term. April 2021, at First Choice Community Healthcare in Albuquerque, New Mexico.

A Friendsgiving dinner for service members and the families of deployed soldiers at Marine Corps Air Station Cherry Point in North Carolina. November 2022.

Touring cancer research programs with Dr. Philip Santangelo of the CUREIT project, far right, and immunologist José Assumpçã at the Emory University Health Sciences Research Building in Atlanta, Georgia. September 2023

My initiative Joining Forces was a cornerstone of the work I did as Second and First Lady. The Military Children's Corner displayed artwork by children from military families in the East Wing hallway. September 2023.

I graded papers whenever I could steal a moment, and wherever I was—here, in the Rose Garden. April 2021.

I had a cutting garden—just like my mom's—planted on the White House grounds so I could take bouquets to people who were sick or just needed cheering up. March 2021.

Celebrating 2024's Teacher Appreciation Week with Becky Pringle, president of the National Education Association, and Randi Weingarten, president of American Federation of Teachers, at the White House.

What a joy to greet *Sesame Street* staff and cast at Kaufman Astoria Studios in Astoria, New York. February 2022.

You're never too old for a first-day-of-school photo. Northern Virginia Community College, fall 2023.

I'm always happiest in a classroom. And who doesn't love a Valentine's Day art project? January 2023, at the South Riva Ridge Child Development Center at Fort Drum, New York.

For the Teacher of the Year state dinner, we used book-themed centerpieces featuring individualized cards for each teacher we celebrated. May 2024, in the East Room of the White House.

My reimagining of the White House public tour featured new interactive display rails. October 2024.

With my grandkids at my favorite place, the beach. From left: Naomi, Finnegan, Hunter, Maisy, and Natalie. April 2019.

Ashley's fortieth birthday party, in the Rose Garden. June 2021.

Little Beau's birthday cake in the tennis pavilion. Thank you, Susie! March 2023.

One of the best days of my life was the White House wedding of my granddaughter Naomi to Peter Neal. November 19, 2022.

Planning for Naomi's wedding was a joy thanks to Bryan Rafanelli—seen here in my East Wing office in fall 2022.

Preparations for Naomi's wedding, with the Washington Monument in background. November 2022.

Joe and I called into the Macy's Thanksgiving Day Parade from Nantucket. November 2022.

Even at the White House, each year Joe and I decorated our family tree with colorful lights and family ornaments. December 2022.

One of our favorite Christmas Eve activities: calling children and keeping tabs on the NORAD Santa Tracker, this year from Camp David. December 2023.

CLOCKWISE: I threw a Philly sweater on over my gown to watch the game before we left for the Kennedy Center Honors. Fly, Eagles, Fly! December 2023.

Family and friends loved to visit us at Camp David, including my sisters Bonny, Kelly, and Kim. November 2024.

Easter Egg Roll in the Jacqueline Kennedy Garden with Office of Management and Budget Director Shalanda Young and her daughter, Charlie. April 2023.

RIGHT: Valentine's Day is one of my favorite holidays—and always a good excuse to set the table in what the kids call "Nana-style."

I love the Olympics! Team USA track and field athlete Gabby Thomas and I recorded a video in Paris from the track. July 2024.

French First Lady Brigitte Macron and I were fast friends. July 2023, at the Élysée Palace in Paris, France.

I saw firsthand the effects of drought and the benefits of US government–funded aid on my visit to a group of Maasai women and girls at the Lositeti outreach site. February 2023, in Kajiado, Kenya.

Joe and I met with Queen Elizabeth II in the Grand Corridor of Windsor Castle. June 2021.

With my prayer partner, Robin Jackson, at Brookland Baptist Church in West Columbia, South Carolina. October 2021.

After the tragic shooting at Robb Elementary in Uvalde, Texas, Joe and I paid our respects to the victims and mourned with their families. May 2022.

Working alongside World Central Kitchen volunteers and North Carolina Governor Roy Cooper in the aftermath of Hurricane Helene, which devastated Asheville. October 2024.

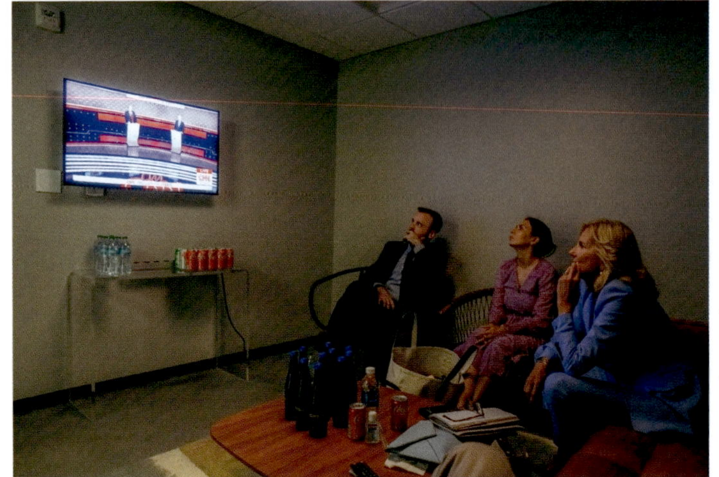

Anthony Bernal took this photo of me with my trip director Marty Browne and my longtime aide Jordan Montoya during Joe's June 2024 debate.

After the debate, supporters came out to greet us at the Hyatt Regency hotel in Atlanta.

We dropped by an Atlanta Waffle House after the debate.

I campaigned hard throughout fall)24 for Vice President Kamala Harris and im Walz. Here I am at ıree Cats restaurant in Clawson, Michigan. October 2024.

Joe, Anthony Bernal, and I prepared to attend the inaugural swearing-in ceremony for the forty-seventh president. January 2025.

Ashley and I said goodbye to the Executive Residence staff on the last day of Joe's presidency. January 2025.

Forever grateful to my family.
Camp David, summer 2024.

For her party, I bought huge metal stars from a garden center and wrapped them with white lights, and I scattered vases all down the table. The menu—Biden-style: a twirl of pasta with thin chicken cutlets. We gathered in the Rose Garden at dusk, and the effect was pretty spectacular. Ashley had mentioned being a huge fan of Mumford & Sons, so I got in touch with Marcus Mumford. I said, "If we flew you over, would you sing at this party?" He did, thrilling everyone.

For Finnegan's and Natalie's graduations, we celebrated at the White House and Camp David. I loved seeing the girls and their friends laughing and having fun, hopeful about their lives ahead.

Throughout our married life, Joe and I always welcomed family and friends to stay in our home. Two of Beau's friends from the University of Pennsylvania lived with us in Wilmington for a summer while they were taking courses. Another kid whose parents were going through a divorce came and stayed for a couple of months. Then my sister Bonny and her cat Mittens lived with me for about a year when she was getting divorced. All three of my children came home again when houses were being renovated or leases were up. There was plenty of room, and I loved to cook for them.

When Naomi was in law school and clerking for Judge Tom Ambro, she lived in Wilmington with us for a while. Then one Sunday, she came back from a weekend in the Hamptons, and she said, "By the way, Nana, on Wednesday I'm going to go to Washington to see a friend, and I'll be back the next morning for work." I noticed a certain flush to her cheeks. She looked a little dazed.

Hmm, I thought. *She met someone she really likes.* I was right—she'd met Peter Neal.

When Naomi and Peter got engaged, there was no question about where we'd want the wedding to take place. It would be one of the highlights of my life. On November 19, 2022, with Bryan Rafanelli, we festooned the White House in white flowers and greenery. When Peter and Naomi stood on the balcony, her veil rippled gently in the wind.

We served a family classic, Hunt's favorite, chicken potpie. The cake was so tall that Naomi had to stand on a ladder to cut it. Hunter said to Peter in his toast, "I could not have hoped for someone that was more brilliant, handsome, loyal, and generous a person for my daughter than you."

There wasn't a dry eye on the South Lawn when Naomi said her vows. She talked about a letter she'd received from her late uncle Beau for her confirmation: "Naomi, I've learned through my life experience that faith is the assurance of things hoped for and the conviction of things not seen. Faith has always carried me. I know it will carry you."

In his toast, Joe said that the White House "had never quite felt like home—until today."

It was true. It was a glorious night.

I think the general assumption is that when you live at the White House, the lavish lifestyle is paid for by the American people. Housing is covered, yes, but there are elaborate protocols ensuring you pay your fair portion. For Naomi's wedding, as well as smaller family parties, that was paid for by us, not taxpayers. If you want to make a birthday cake in the White House kitchen, you have to pay for the flour—as well as the sugar, the salt, the eggs, and all the other ingredients. If you want it boxed up for transit, you need to pay for the box. That's only fair, of course. There are also considerable subsidies for White House residents. You're not paying the salary of the White House chef who will offer to whip the cake up for you. (Thank goodness, because Susie's cakes are so amazing they would be worth millions!)

When you're out at a restaurant, there's usually a military valet who is in charge and trained in food security. They post in the kitchen to make sure that the president's food isn't being poisoned. They manage the waitstaff, and they pay the bill for you—but if it's a meal you've chosen to go out for, you do have to reimburse for it. Everything is routinely reconciled so that you are paying for what you consume.

There were also elaborate rules surrounding gifts. When people visited the White House, they often brought presents. Sometimes little things—flowers, wine—but sometimes big ones, like the 7.5-carat synthetic diamond Indian Prime Minister Narendra Modi handed me at his state visit—a symbol of his country's bid to become a leader in lab-grown gems. The diamond was gorgeous. But it wasn't given to me, technically. It was given to the First Lady, which meant it belonged to the federal government. As soon as something was given to me with a possible value of more than $480, the gift watchdog would snatch it out of my hands before I had a chance to so much as try it on. Their job was to catalog and assess the value of every present. I was allowed to purchase the gifts that were given to me if I paid fair market price.

In the case of Modi's diamond, the prime minister said that it had been handmade in his hometown for $2,500. He even had the bill of sale. I thought, *Maybe I'll buy it.* Then the State Department appraised it at $20,000, so I did not. I was told I could display it in my office or borrow it to wear. So I had it put in a ring setting and wore it to official functions. When we left office, I gave it back. The ring went into a warehouse along with an infinitude of other presidential gifts, many of which are simply destroyed.

I was given a brooch by Ukraine made out of bomb shrapnel, which to me seemed priceless, but the gift enforcers still put one on it: $14,063.

I let myself buy my favorite gift. When Brigitte Macron came to the state dinner we gave for her, she gave me a delicate little bracelet that she knew I would love. Because she had picked it out for me, it had sentimental value. I paid the State Department so I could take it with me when we left office. I still wear it every day, and it reminds me each time I look at it of the intricate ballet of hosting at the White House.

CHAPTER 22

For eight years, my social secretary Carlos Elizondo and I had decorated the vice president's residence for the holidays, so I had a sense of what the season meant in Washington. However, the First Lady's work as a hostess became all-consuming every December. We hosted the Kennedy Center Honors, followed by the Congressional Holiday Ball with two thousand members of Congress and their families, and then the festivities really began—some twenty-five parties and receptions per season. We greeted everyone from Girl Scouts to football players, tech CEOs to civil servants. I loved this time of year.

Fortunately, we had lots of help on the decorating front. In November, about three hundred volunteers came from all over the country, at their own expense, to decorate the White House for the holiday season. They worked for three or four days from seven in the morning till seven at night. Friends and family members I know who've done this affectionately call it "adult camp." They wore bedecked aprons and jingle bell necklaces and Santa hats, and they glue-gunned their hearts out while making friends for life.

The groups were chosen by application, and many of the same people returned again and again each year. Without them, it would have been nearly impossible to prepare all the rooms in time for the usual crush of one hundred thousand visitors. Someone was in charge of each of the dozen or so rooms and halls. In the course of that week, I'd overhear things like: "Your snowball isn't big enough. *Do it again.*"

Once my sisters Kim and Kelly heard about the decorating, they were all in! The moment they'd finished their Thanksgiving dinners, they hopped in the car and drove to DC. They didn't tell anyone they were my sisters, but eventually some people found out because they knew the staff so well. When the Christmas special was on television, we'd watch to see if we could catch a glimpse of Kim or Kelly on a ladder or wielding a mean glue gun.

Each year, we started planning for Christmas in early February; staff would buy the decorations in August. Then we'd reveal the decorations the Monday after Thanksgiving. There was a press preview at 5:30 in the morning, with a military band playing holiday music throughout. Every room—the library, the Red Room, the Blue Room, the China Room—needed to be decorated within the theme. So that everyone who went on the Christmas tour would feel joy and inspiration, my staff and I spent months planning the experience.

As a rule, I wanted the holidays to bring people together, so my overarching theme was unity. I made sure to make it feel as homey as possible, with handprint ornaments by military families and personal recipes from volunteers. I also wanted to evoke all the senses. One year, we had a model train blowing a whistle on its track around the tree; another, we had artistic lighting that made it look as if a star over one of the entrances was rotating.

In 2021, I chose the theme "Gifts from the Heart," which honored gifts like service and faith. The goal was to celebrate unity and healing in the wake of COVID. We encircled the Blue Room tree with messages of goodwill.

Because we couldn't invite anyone in person to the White House that year, we worked with PBS to record *In Performance at the White House: Spirit of the Season*. Our friend Jennifer Garner hosted the evening, which included Camila Cabello, Eric Church, the Jonas Brothers, Norah Jones, Pentatonix, and Billy Porter. The Northwell Health Nurse Choir and Voices of Service made the show extra meaningful. Andrea Bocelli, along with his son Matteo and young daughter, Virginia, sang "O Holy Night" and "Hallelujah." Joe told him his favorite was Bocelli's moving "Fall on Me." I didn't request it for the special because I thought Joe wouldn't be able to get through it without becoming emotional. So Bocelli sang it especially for Joe, a magical moment the two of them spent together, one singing and one listening in rapture, tears in his eyes.

In 2022, the White House holiday theme was "We the People." I used mirror ornaments so viewers would see themselves looking back at the decorations. The Blue Room tree featured state birds from all fifty states. There was a gingerbread replica of Philadelphia's Independence Hall. The State Dining Room held self-portrait ornaments made by students of the Teachers of the Year. We also unveiled the first official White House menorah, which was made by the resident carpentry shop, headed by Robbie Thompson. Yet what everyone seemed to love best were the simple cotton balls hanging from the ceiling in the East Colonnade to represent snow.

For Christmas 2023, my favorite year, we went with the theme

"Magic, Wonder, and Joy." To create wonder, we made it look like a tree was coming out of the East Wing. We invited the National Confectioners Association to sponsor displays for the decor. They outdid themselves! They created huge gingerbread men, candy canes, gumdrops, and ice cream cones hanging from the ceiling. Santa's sleigh flew through the foyer. What a joy to see the children's reactions as they walked through those rooms!

Even though we were in the White House, I tried to maintain as many of our Delaware holiday traditions as I could. "Santa" always added snow to the boughs of our Christmas tree when he delivered gifts. A mixture of Ivory Snow and water does the trick. Blair Downing, the White House chief usher, asked that Santa take extra care with the snow given that a Rothko was hanging nearby. On Christmas mornings, I cooked the grandchildren their favorite holiday breakfast, bacon-and-egg sandwiches.

One year we installed an ice rink on the South Lawn. The last time there had been ice skating there was in 1980, when the Carters put one up and invited Peggy Fleming to perform. The night we unveiled the rink, we were honored by performances by Olympic gold medalist Brian Boitano and even *Snoopy on Ice*.

I do know how to skate. I skated on frozen canals in New Hope, Pennsylvania, with my family; attended Ice Capades with my grandmother (the pennant graced my wall for years of my childhood); and took ice skating as one of my electives as a University of Delaware undergrad. At the White House skating rink opening, I was gifted a beautiful pair of custom pink skates by Dan Riegelman of Riedell Skates. Still, I did not have enough faith in my ability to guarantee that I would not take a spill and get a concussion. That would not have been festive, especially in front of Snoopy. I wore boots out onto the ice, and I held Brian Boitano's hand.

"Children have something to teach us, if we are wise enough to listen," I told the crowd. "How to remain present, even as a busy world beckons us. How to open ourselves up to love and wonder, and to marvel at every moment, no matter how ordinary."

CHAPTER 23

Over the winter holidays in 2023, Joe and I took a couple of the grandchildren with us on vacation to Saint Croix. On New Year's Day, Joe and I woke up Natalie and Hunter to watch the sunrise. We took a selfie—in the photo, Joe and I look *way* more thrilled than the kids—and the grandchildren crawled back to bed. Joe and I stayed up and talked about what lay ahead.

We'd spent Christmas at the White House. People in Washington seemed more optimistic about the direction the country was going in, and confident in Joe's leadership. During the 2020 race, Joe had privately floated the idea of voluntarily being a one-term, transitional president, but as he explored the question of a reelection bid, every one of his senior advisors insisted he needed to run.

By many metrics, things were far better halfway through Joe's term than they'd been when he entered office. There had been buzz around various candidates as possible primary contenders against Joe if he decided to leave after one term, but we were told that based on the polling, Joe was the Democrats' best bet. The stakes were extremely high. The Supreme Court had struck down *Roe v. Wade* in June; lawmakers on the right were signaling that it was just the beginning of a rollback of women's access to health care. I'd heard horrible stories from women denied care for life-threatening situations such as ectopic pregnancies, fetal anomalies guaranteed to result in stillbirth, and miscarriages in progress. Women were being left to bleed until they were about to die from sepsis before it was legally safe for a doctor to step in. They might be told to sit in hospital parking lots, waiting for a fetal heartbeat to fully stop, before they could be admitted.

In the 2022 midterms, Democrats had held the Senate. Republicans had won control of the House, but the margin was very slim. It was one of the best midterm showings in decades for the incumbent's party. While the age question was there, Joe kept showing that he was still able to do the job.

Still, Joe wanted to be sure that running again would be the right thing, especially for the family. I floated a hypothetical: "I've wondered if the Republicans would continue to go after our family if you decided not to run?"

Joe didn't think that was a good reason to run or not run, whether the other side would continue to attack us.

Four years earlier, in the lead-up to the 2019 campaign, the grandkids called a family meeting to encourage Joe to run. Naomi gathered us all in Wilmington. Joe was concerned about the effect of the campaign on the grandchildren in particular. The online discourse was brutal.

Our grandson Hunter took out his phone, scrolled for a minute, and then held out the phone. On it was a post from an extremist site with a photo of Joe kissing him. It appeared to be a kiss on the lips. The article suggested that this was evidence of child abuse.

"If we can survive terrible lies like this," Hunter said, "we can survive anything. You should run, Pop. They can't say anything worse."

My family believed that Joe was the right person for the job.

To me, Joe was definitely aging, but he was not exhibiting signs of dementia or senility. In November 2020, he had twisted his ankle tripping over one of the dogs at our home in Rehoboth Beach. He was diagnosed with hairline fractures in his foot. He was given a walking boot, but he opted not to wear it. As a result, the foot did not heal properly. Now you're not only aging, but you're aging with a damaged foot. I kept saying, "Why can't we break it again and set it straight?" But apparently it was more a problem with the soft tissue.

While the fractures healed, the nerves had been affected, which meant he was in excruciating pain most days and there was nothing to do about it but rest—something he refused to do. In spite of the pain, he would stand for hours and hours. He has always had a high pain threshold, but that was a lot even for him. I'd look over sometimes during a holiday party or a long receiving line and see on his face that he was suffering.

Still, Joe was the same man I'd always known. He'd always been an athlete, and he was determined to keep it up. It was hard for him to admit that he couldn't be as physically active as he'd always been, and he refused to give up longtime athletic pursuits like biking. He was a believer in baseball player Satchel Paige's line "Age is a case of mind over matter. If you don't mind, it don't matter." Joe also loved the quote "You're only as old as you think you are!" As a onetime college football player, he wanted to keep jogging onto the stage into his eighties. The kids and I begged him to stop. But the more we told him not to, the more he did it, just to prove that he could.

Physically, he was no longer 100 percent. For that matter, I wasn't either. I used to wear five-inch heels without a second thought. By my seventies, I still wore heels, though they tended to be a bit shorter. Joe was just older. Even if he threw on a pair of Ray-Ban sunglasses, he was part of a generation that preferred hours-long speeches to short videos. Still, there was such a disconnect between who Joe was to me and how the world saw him. A recent visitor watched Joe head out the door, hop into his dark green 1967 Corvette Stingray, rev the engine, and screech down the driveway.

"*That*," the visitor said, "is sure not the guy they portray on television."

Even if he had slowed down in the years before his reelection bid, I believed in my heart that he was still good enough and wise enough and capable enough to govern. He never wavered from his values, the same ones I grew up with. I believe that if his health had ever deteriorated to the point where he was no longer able to serve, he would have had the humility to admit that—and if he were to step down before the end of a second term, he would have handed the reins to Kamala.

For the good of the country, I knew that I, for one, would rather Joe have a second term than not. There was a lot of good work to be done. Given what terrible things Joe's opponent guaranteed he would do, the choice seemed clear. I felt that Joe was a far, far better option than his opponent—who, by the way, was only three years younger than Joe.

In spite of his age, Joe was still doing the job, and doing it well. In February 2023, he and I were out for dinner at the Red Hen in DC when he told me he'd be secretly leaving the White House in the middle of the night. When we were out together in public, people were often trying to read our lips. They almost always got it wrong, but it was still uncomfortable to be watched that closely, and to know that whatever people thought they picked up would be in the papers the next day. So when Joe shared a major bit of news partway through our meal, he covered his mouth with his napkin and spoke softly.

"Tonight, after we get home," he said, "I'm going on a mission to Ukraine."

I nodded. While I knew the region was dangerous, I had complete faith that Joe would be okay because I had full confidence in the Secret Service and our military.

At four that morning, he made his way to the airport in a baseball cap, getting on a plane for Poland. After landing, he took the train to Ukraine to meet with President Zelensky. I knew there was a team down in the Presidential Emergency Operations Center (PEOC) bunkers monitoring Joe's trip, so I went to see how he was doing and brought them pizza. When Joe returned, I went with him to visit the special ops team, to thank them for all they had done to keep him safe.

President Zelensky called the surprise visit "historic, timely, brave." He said that it was "an extremely important sign of support for all Ukrainians," as well as "the most important visit in the entire history of Ukraine–US relations."

Joe had taken a risky, physically demanding, clandestine trip, and it had been a great success—further evidence that in spite of his age he was still very much up to the job.

CHAPTER 24

In May 2023, I attended King Charles III's coronation—the first such occasion in seventy years. To make it more meaningful, Finnegan accompanied me on the once-in-a-lifetime trip. As a history major at U. Penn, she was poised to appreciate it all.

We had our fascinators ready, and yet it wasn't until I was on the flight to London that it actually hit me that I was going. The prior week, I'd thrown the South Korea state dinner, welcomed the president of the Philippines, hosted the Combatant Commanders dinner, administered final exams, and posted final grades. As with so many historic moments in those four years, I was running so fast I barely had time to take any of it in.

I'd been to the UK several times before as a Senate spouse and as Second Lady. On my first foreign trip as First Lady, in June 2021, I attended a cocktail reception in Cornwall with the royal family before having dinner with the G7 participants. The reception was held at the Eden Project's magnificent rainforest and Mediterranean biodomes in Cornwall, where Queen Elizabeth told Joe that her husband had not wanted to live to be one hundred, declaring it "too old." Duchess of Cornwall Camilla Parker Bowles told me she was happy to see someone her age there, because so many of the spouses were younger. I told her we were probably the only ones who were Beatles fans when they were still together.

At the dinner, I noticed how creative the menu was—melon soup with pansy blossoms (edible!), fresh turbot, roasted potatoes and spinach, a cheese course, a meringue with ice cream, and then mini ice cream cones (Joe, ice cream enthusiast that he is, ate three).

The conversation between Joe and British Prime Minister Boris Johnson centered around the challenges in getting people vaccinated, Putin and his agenda, childcare, the Social Security system—but when they started outgunning each other with obscure statistics, I stopped listening. *This is what happens when you get a bunch of politicians together for what's supposed to be a party*, I thought. *The charts come out.*

Prime Minister Boris Johnson's wife, Carrie, and I had decided to go for a walk earlier that day. She awakened her baby, Wilfred, so he could join us. I was amazed by how little he seemed to mind—any baby I've ever woken up has been outraged. As we walked down to the water together, Wilfred on her hip, Carrie told me she was shy with the press and asked me how I managed. My answer: You just get used to it, and try your best not to let it affect you. And there are always opportunities to send a positive message—I was wearing my LOVE jacket to signal warmth toward our allies.

At every event we'd been at together, Kate and William were friendly. When Princess Kate and I cooed over rabbits at a primary school in West Cornwall, I found her instantly likeable, very unassuming. She made me feel at ease. She seemed so grounded. I encouraged her to keep a journal about her experiences. She said she liked to draw and paint, but I said you can never have too many ways to privately express your feelings.

Joe and I both looked forward to tea with Queen Elizabeth. After flying to Windsor Castle by helicopter, we were taken to survey the troops inside the courtyard. This is customary in the UK, and American presidents offer the same presentation when heads of state visit the United States.

After posing for a photo, we followed the queen to the elevator to take us to the second floor. It was just the three of us. British protocol had advised us not to talk about family since her husband, Prince Philip, had died just a few months prior, at the age of ninety-nine.

So I studiously did not ask the queen about her husband or anything related to the royal family. As soon as we began speaking, though, she filled us in on her eleven great-grandchildren and the new one on the way. I was amazed that she poured the tea herself and wanted to talk about foreign policy. She had two new Corgi puppies to help her through the hard times. One came in, and she gave him half a smoked salmon tea sandwich.

Her personal living room was filled with photograph after photograph of members of her family. There was nothing stiff or stuffy about the room, but it held a quiet elegance—much like the queen herself.

We gazed through the large windows to the wing on the other side of the courtyard. Queen Elizabeth remarked that it was quite busy over there, but her wing was rather hushed.

I think she and Joe could have gone on talking forever. She had such a wonderful sense of curiosity about people and world events. She was rather honest about some leaders she disapproved of, and I felt grateful to be taken into her confidence.

As we were about to leave, someone came in and presented us with a small box of freshly picked strawberries from the garden and a bunch of red souvenir pencils with gold crowns at the top.

On my 2023 trip to London with Finnegan, I got to know the new prime minister, Rishi Sunak, and his wife, Akshata Narayana Murty. Akshata hosted me for a military families event at 10 Downing Street—a sign of our strong NATO alliance. It was fun getting to know her. Akshata even came to a cycle class with me—SoulCycle diplomacy.

As Finnegan and I approached Westminster Abbey for the coronation, trumpets sounded out. Heads of state and royalty from all over the globe were arriving to affirm the importance of leadership and unity and traditions. Even countries without a monarchy had sent representatives, all of them seeming eager to participate in this moment honoring the sacred nature of leadership. While the coronation was a grand event, it had a touch of melancholy because what occasioned it was Elizabeth's passing.

Seeing the crowns placed on the heads of Charles and Camilla at Westminster Abbey, I felt that I was watching history being made. The royal I'd known best up to that point was Prince Harry. I'd liked him instantly when I met him in 2012 at a reception for wounded US and British troops. He was so friendly and respectful to everyone there. In 2014 in England and 2016 in Orlando, we'd had a good time together at the international Invictus Games, a competition he founded for wounded warriors, and he'd come to the White House when Barack was president. I was thinking about Harry when I felt a tap on my arm.

"How can they call Pop old?" Finny said with regards to Joe. "Look at most of the leaders." She gestured toward the leaders of Ireland, Italy, Finland, Sweden . . .

I gave her a little hug and straightened her fascinator.

CHAPTER 25

"Your job will be terminated in two weeks," read the college president's letter, hand-delivered by the provost. I stared at the paper in shock. I had signed my usual annual contract just a few months earlier, in July 2023. It was now winter. The reason I was given for my dismissal was financial. To avoid a conflict with the Constitution's Emoluments Clause, designed to prevent elected officials from accepting money or benefits that might sway them politically, I had been paid through a grant. According to the letter, the grant was used up. I had to clean out my desk.

To be fired so abruptly was devastating. I wanted to at least have a conversation with the college president before I left. I'd been teaching at Northern Virginia Community College for fifteen years, ever since the dean at the time, Jimmie McClellan, had courted me and convinced me to join the faculty in 2009. In the letter, the college's new president did not express any regret. There was no trace of doubt, no "I'm sorry this happened. We value you as a faculty member." When White House staff tried to get in touch with her, she was out of town and their calls went unanswered.

I felt sick. I was hosting holiday parties at the White House, so

I had to go from seeing emails about my firing to groups of children belting out "Jingle Bells." I was all festive energy and "Merry Christmas!" on the outside, but on the inside, I was mourning the loss of a job that I loved, and that I believed made a difference.

I admired my students so much. What they were going through to be in that classroom! They took nothing for granted. The last semester I was there, I had one student who was living in a motel room with her three kids. I found it heartbreaking when she dropped out halfway through the semester.

Once, when teaching a class on writing about conflict, I purchased Google Cardboard headsets so that the class could experience global conflicts in 3D. Most of the students loved the new technology and said that they felt as though they were there. Except that it turned out one of my students had been there in Syria, and she ran out of the room sobbing. I ran after her into the ladies' room, where she told me her story. She'd left her family back in Syria and married an American; she was basically alone here. It was heart-wrenching. We became friends. We still text, and she sends me pictures of her boys in Halloween costumes and Christmas outfits. I'm so proud of her.

My students knew me as "Dr. B." The only real evidence that I had another life was that they had to go through a metal detector to get into my classroom. I worked with the Secret Service agents to create as much normalcy as possible. They monitored the class on video from another room and had me wear a panic fob on a lanyard (I bedazzled it with stick-on jewels).

I loved teaching. One program I'd started at NOVA was the Women's Retention Group. Our goal was to help ease the special burdens on many women that kept them from succeeding at college—for example, the middle-aged woman returning to school after a divorce and having to navigate childcare, or the young woman with profound math anxiety who needed tutoring but wasn't sure how to access it. We arranged for space where women could nurse their babies, and we gave them access to mental health services. There were benches outside where they could meditate surrounded by beautiful flowers.

One of my mentees was Roxy, a woman from Ukraine. She'd tell me, "Dr. B., I was on the phone last night with my mom, and we were talking through the bombs." There was a room on campus where the mentors and their mentees could have a cup of tea and just talk. I had lunch with Roxy almost every month. We still text. Some people come into your life and bring you joy when you least expect it. Roxy is that person for me. I always look forward to seeing her and hearing all the challenges she's taken on. She's wicked smart—and has a fabulous sense of style, right down to her five-inch platform heels. I distinctly remember her first day walking into class in a short pink outfit, pink shoes, and pink hair. She hasn't changed in the many years I've known her.

Often on the first day of class, I told my students—there were usually twenty or twenty-two—we'd be doing a poetry assignment, and they'd all groan loudly. Most of my students were going to school for tech jobs. I taught a lot of nursing assistants, EMTs, IT majors—they were often coming to my classroom straight before or after dropping a child off at school or going to work, wearing scrubs or coveralls, trying to stay awake after working a night shift.

"A *poem*?" one whined, as if I'd told them to wash the windows.

Ignoring their protests, I said, "I'm going to read this poem to you, and I want you to talk about it."

Then I shared the poem "Where I'm From," by George Ella

Lyon. It begins: "I am from clothespins, / from Clorox and carbon-tetrachloride. / I am from the dirt under the back porch."

We began to talk about where each student was from and what images they might use to represent their homelands—how they celebrated the holidays, what flowers grew in their gardens, what food their mothers made them when they were sick. Then I had them write their own poems. While I had high hopes for their work, even I was so proud of the papers they turned in that week. Their "I am from" poems were heartfelt and sparse, but powerful. By incorporating all the senses, they conveyed the richness of their cultures, and the deep pride they took in their families and in how far they'd come.

"I'm from fried plantain and cassava dough, / whole wheat bread and tea."

"I'm from the long deployments . . . I am from kids playing in streets, / walking to the shoppette and PX."

"I come from freshly made tortillas."

"I am . . . from where good was never good enough and big was never big enough."

"I'm from where the first homo sapiens walked."

"I am from posadas in January . . . I am first to step foot in college / from the ink on sturdy books."

Reading these poems, I could feel my chest swell with admiration. Beneath their grades (10/10!), I wrote words of encouragement like "You work hard in my class. You will be successful because you have guts and perseverance." Every time I told my students that they would do well, it was almost as if I were trying to cast a spell on them: *You WILL excel. You WILL have a bright future. You WILL go far.* If only I could make that true by wishing for it. The reality was they all had huge obstacles to overcome. I spent as much time worrying about their home lives as about lesson plans. I felt that it was my job to give them confidence and build them up.

At the next class after giving the poem assignment, I said, "Who wants to read their poem?" Hands shot up all around the room. Inside of a week, they'd gone from hating the whole idea of a poem to wanting to read their own poetry in front of the class. As each student finished reading, they'd startle to the sound of everyone clapping for them, and I'd see a huge smile spread over their face. They seemed to feel so good about what they did.

In fact, during one class, the students notified me that they wanted to hang the poems up in the classroom. Usually college classroom walls are bare, but I got out construction paper and tape and made a display out of the poems as if we were a kindergarten class that had just laminated fall leaves. In that moment, we created community. Looking at the poems on the wall, somebody would say, "Hey, I'm from Peru, too!" Or "My grandmother cooks the same dish!" From there, meaningful friendships grew.

Whatever the group's makeup, it didn't take long for the class to form a community. Nobody was sitting there smirking or rolling their eyes. When you teach English, you learn more about your students than you do teaching other subjects, I think. They seemed to trust me, and in their journal assignments, they'd talk about going through a rough patch with a partner or finding themselves unexpectedly pregnant.

One student who had been in foster care came to class and cried every single day. She had no one. She'd come to Virginia with her boyfriend, who then broke up with her. She struggled to stay in school. My class's writing tutor, Paula, took her under her wing. She invited her to her home for holidays and helped her manage the educational system.

All it took was one person who cared about and mentored her through the rough times. It took her several years to get her degree, but she did it. She moved to Texas with her new boyfriend, and now she has a whole extended family that loves her. Thanks in no small part to Paula.

Teachers have so much to do every minute, but somehow they manage to give that kind word or compliment that brightens a student's day. It says, *You're special. You can do this.* You have to know how. That's what we do as teachers. It's all about building confidence, listening, supporting, and providing a space for them to make connections.

I watched every year as they'd start to trust one another. As I packed up my bag at the end of class, I loved to hear them reach out to one another: "Would you like a ride to the bus?" "Can I call you to talk through the homework?"

For another journal assignment, I said, "If a meteor was heading toward the earth and you had five minutes left, what would be the last song you'd want to hear?" They'd have to think about that and then write about their song. I let them share their songs and explain their choice to the class. They loved that assignment, perhaps in part because it gave them permission to blast music in school. My meteor song showed my age—it was the gentle hymn "Be Not Afraid," a song that Beau loved. The chorus promises: "I go before you always / Come, follow me and I will give you rest." To me, that was far more soothing a possible final song than the window-rattling ones they chose, but I suppose in an apocalypse scenario the heart wants what it wants.

I kept my life as a political spouse separate from my life on campus, with very rare exceptions. In 2019, I went on Trevor Noah's show. For years, I'd been teaching his memoir, *Born a Crime*, and we had group discussions about his childhood in South Africa and how he had developed resilience. And in 2010, I was asked to introduce Barack

Obama when he spoke on campus about a bill designed to fix issues with the ACA and with the student loan system. The students seemed to forgive me for those two moments of worlds colliding.

In the end, the issue that had led to my termination was easily resolved, and I kept my position. I didn't want to create a problem with the faculty, so I only told one or two other people at the school.

When I see former students now, whether running into them out in the world or via photos and texts they still send me regularly, I'm often taken aback. They're so *old*. Some of my students who were just out of high school when I taught them are now middle-aged! In my memory, they're still fresh-faced college kids. Every time I hear one of their meteor songs, I think of the thousands of students I taught over the years—and how they made me laugh. Whatever else was happening in the world or in the rest of my life, teaching truly brought me joy. Every day, I miss the structure of teaching, and I miss my students.

I taught my last class at NOVA in December 2024. Disappointingly, after I left, school administrators said that all students had to be included in NOVA's Women's Retention Group, including men, and the mission of the group became so diluted that it no longer served the same purpose. At least the garden remains to this day, with female professors still dragging out the hoses regularly to tend to it.

After teaching for more than half my life, it was a hard decision to leave. It was so strange knowing that after forty years, I was walking away from the classroom, maybe for the last time. Fortunately, fate brought me the perfect ending to my teaching career. As I've said, what I tried to do most of all was give my students confidence. I learned that a young man in the class, a bassist, had to give a concert to raise money for his music class, and he was petrified.

A boxer named Archie Moore once said, “I ride my fear like a fast horse.” I knew that the student just needed to get on the horse and it would carry him through. I suggested he use our class as a rehearsal. I had him come in as if it was the event, and with the class’s support, I coached him through it.

“This is so exciting for us to hear you do this!” I told him.

He’d been dragging his bass into the classroom every day. It was like another member of the class. We were thrilled that he’d be sharing his talent with us, and that we could possibly help him get over his nerves.

As soon as he finished the classical piece, we erupted into applause and cheers. The young man looked dazed. He grew visibly taller, almost as if he were a parched plant being watered. He left to go and give his concert with more confidence than he would have had otherwise. My work was done. I turned off the lights in the classroom and walked out into the next chapter of my life.

CHAPTER 26

My work ethic comes from my father. Hard work is in my nature, whether in the classroom, out on the campaign trail, or in the execution of my duties as First Lady. Traveling internationally via an Air Force plane referred to as Bright Star when the First Lady is on board (a plane is only called Air Force One when the president is the one flying on it), we would need to stop periodically so the plane could be refueled. We could stop at the same places each time and never leave the plane, or we could use the stop as an opportunity to connect with more people. Two times we did this that I'll never forget were stops in Alaska and Italy.

On our way to Hiroshima, Japan, in May 2023 for the forty-ninth G7 summit, I chose to highlight the issue of broadband internet expansion with a visit to Bethel, a tiny, remote town in western Alaska with a mostly Alaska Native Yup'ik population.

During the campaign, Joe had talked about shining a bright light on inequity. He'd vowed not to forget the small towns that had suffered neglect—and he hadn't. One of the ways that Joe kept that promise was to make a huge push to connect everyone in America via high-speed broadband internet. I don't think it's possible to realize the impact of broadband until you visit these communities and see what it means to go from being completely cut off from the rest of the world to having access to telehealth, to education, to remote work.

Native American communities were often overlooked. Joe made them a priority. He hired the first Native American cabinet secretary, Deb Haaland, who served as secretary of the interior. Showing up matters, so I was proud to travel to the First Nations nine times. They had been so neglected for so long, and we'd seen how much of a difference could be made, particularly in terms of public health and infrastructure. In 2021, I visited a COVID vaccination clinic in the Navajo Nation with my friends President Jonathan Nez and his wife, Phefelia.

That trip to Bethel, Alaska, was a visceral moment of connection between our administration and a community that had sometimes felt forgotten by the federal government. When we arrived, it seemed as though every single person in town showed up to greet us. The advance teams were invigorated, because it was very rare that you go into a region that had never been visited by a president or First Lady. I wore a traditional qaspeq jacket in red, white, and blue that had been given to me by the local designer Letha Chimegalrea Simon.

"With high-speed internet," I told the crowd assembled at the high school, "you'll have better access to critical health care, new educational tools, and remote job opportunities. It will change lives. It will save lives. And it will help make our world a little brighter, a little more beautiful."

I was so moved by the local name that had been given to the broadband project: Airraq, which I was told is Yup'ik for "a string that tells a story." How perfect is that? Infrastructure programs such as this one that Joe made happen had truly profound effects. For this rural community, the stories of the world would now be so much more available to them, and it would be that much easier for them to share their amazing culture with the rest of us.

My final foreign trip as First Lady in December 2024 was to Abu Dhabi and Qatar, accompanied by Ashley. We realized that a good fuel stop en route to Abu Dhabi would be at the US Naval Air Station at Sigonella, Italy, which was near my ancestral homeland of Gesso—my father's family came to America from Sicily around 1900.

We began by meeting with military families to honor their service. I spoke to about 150 service members and their families as part of my Joining Forces initiative to support the family members, caregivers, and survivors of our military.

"We have just begun the holiday season at the White House," I told them. "And I hope to bring some of that warmth across the ocean to all of you—though you seem to have created a pretty incredible display here, too. This year—Sigonella's sixty-fifth anniversary—you've shown the world why you're the 'Hub of the Med.'"

I praised some of their many accomplishments, which included a record score in a problem-solving evaluation, the most community relations events of any base, their perfect soccer season, and their ability to weave daily through the Sicilian traffic.

We then drove to Gesso. As I was the first Italian American First Lady, Gesso took pride in my family roots. When we arrived, we saw that people had hung welcome banners from their balconies. They showed me the church where my great-great-grandmother had been baptized. There was music. There was drinking. The mayor brought me a bouquet of flowers.

At one point when everyone we met was calling us their cousins and hugging us, Ashley whispered, "Mom, they don't look much like us, do they?" I agreed that the resemblance was slight, but we kept hugging them like family.

At a church we visited there was an etching of Gesso's sister city, Hammonton, New Jersey, where my mother and father grew up and where I was born. I was moved thinking about how happy they would have been to see me visiting our homeland. I spoke to the crowd about how my great-grandparents were shaped by Italian values: loyalty, hard work, and the belief that there's always room for one more seat at the table.

CHAPTER 27

"How do we do a domestic stop before you go abroad since you're going to lose a week of campaigning?" my chief of staff, Anthony Bernal, asked me as we planned out my travel schedule for June 2024. "We're going to France next week, that's why it's really important that we get to Erie, Pennsylvania, for their community college commencement. So if you're there already, you might as well go to the Pittsburgh Pride festival. Because why not? There's the Congressional Picnic you can hit on the way to the airport. Then we'll get you to Paris for the state dinner and Normandy trip—you can shower at the airport."

Anthony and I worked well together, because when it came to logistics, we were both insane. Campaigning, we often did seven stops in three days, determined to make the most of our time and reach the greatest number of people. We figured out how to manage our trips down to the minute. But we would look back on that week in June when, in addition to the rest, Hunter was on trial—for having misrepresented his drug use on a gun application and owning a gun while using illegal drugs—as the mad dash that almost broke us.

June 3

The week began on my birthday, June 3. I spent it at the Wilmington courthouse for Hunter's jury selection. I'd been in and around that building many times, for jury duty and when Joe's Senate office had been close by, but never had I been so invested in an outcome—and never had the air-conditioning been blasting so unrelentingly.

The day was hot and stormy, which made entering the cold, dark courthouse especially grim. The perspiration inside my dark purple pantsuit turned clammy against my skin as I made my way into the courtroom through a throng of press shouting and taking pictures.

Hunter knew I was coming, but beyond that, I'd told almost no one that I would be attending, so people seemed surprised when I showed up. One side of the courtroom was filled with well-wishers. When I reached those benches, I saw Hunter's wife Melissa, Ashley, and many of Hunt's friends. There were a number of kind ministers from the community praying over us. One took my hand and said, "Joy comes in the morning."

Moments like those kept me going, as did some of the quotations I'd collected in my journals. I thought of a line from Abraham Verghese's novel *The Covenant of Water*: "Faith is to know the pattern is there, even though none is visible."

On the other side was a wall of press staring at us, notebooks at the ready.

It could be hard to stay calm. Certain members of the press yelled questions like "How are you feeling, Jill?"

How do you think I feel? I wanted to say. *My heart is broken.*

That day, Ashley, Melissa, and I and everyone else in our group tried to take every break we could. We'd get sandwiches from Janssen's

Market and sit in the courtyard of the Quoin hotel to thaw out from the freezing courtroom.

As the selection began, I settled onto a hard bench and tried to see Hunter through the eyes of the jury—six men, six women, racially diverse. The lawyers had bios on them and knew who had addiction in their family and what people's feelings were about drugs. But beyond that, it was hard to know how they would react. Would they see him as a spoiled rich kid? Would they feel empathy with him? Would they respect him for having been to hell and come out the other side, committed to his sobriety, with a stable life and a young child?

He went into dangerous neighborhoods, handed strangers thousands of dollars. Sometimes those strangers returned with drugs; sometimes they didn't. The details were so salacious—all these drugs, all this money, all these women. The lurid images of him with his shirt off, pipe hanging from his lips, the amount of risk he was taking—it was almost as if he were taunting death. Would that make a mother on the jury more likely to feel protective and show him leniency or be horrified and make sure he was punished? It was so beyond anyone's normal life. How would the jurors make sense of it?

June 4

On the first day of testimony in Hunter's trial, I sat behind him, in the front row between Ashley and Melissa. The prosecutor said that Hunter had lied on a gun-purchase form and that no one was above the law. Hunter's lawyer, Abbe Lowell, said that Hunter misunderstood the form and was drinking but not actively using drugs at the time.

Sitting on the hard bench, I thought back on a conversation I'd had with Hunter when the news came out that he'd been charged.

"Why did you buy a *gun*?" I asked. I was flooded with questions: *Why would he ever want a gun? Was he in some sort of danger? What was he thinking?*

When I thought of guns, I thought of people I knew growing up in Pennsylvania. My mother's father, who owned a drugstore, was a duck hunter. At dinner, we had to pick the buckshot out of our teeth when we ate. My father had a gun in his nightstand in case of intruders. The men in my family who served in the military knew their way around rifles. But my main association with guns was a neighbor, a doctor, who built a duck blind by our man-made lake. He would invite his doctor friends over. They would get into fatigues, and they would hide behind their hay bales until a duck or a goose had the misfortune to come by, and then they would blast away. It seemed so crazy to me. We lived in a neighborhood with a school. Children lived around the lake, including the doctor's! But why would Hunter have a gun? In a city? It made no sense to me.

"I was getting a coffee," Hunter told me when I asked him to explain what happened. "I looked out the window and I saw a gun shop. I decided to buy one."

During the time after Joe and I learned that Hunter was battling addiction, we tried to become a refuge for the rest of the family, a neutral party. Joe was the family cheerleader, the person calling everyone daily, checking in. I was the navigator, negotiator, manager, truth-teller, trying to manage all the dynamics. I wanted my grandchildren to know that I understood if they were struggling, and I wanted them to feel comfortable talking to me.

One complex family dynamic was Hunter's relationship with his brother's widow, Hallie. She was with him through some of the most difficult years of his addiction, and she was called to testify at the trial. I'd always known Hallie to be thoughtful and methodical, but apparently, when she'd seen the weapon, she'd panicked. Rather than turning it in to authorities, she drove to Janssen's and threw it in the trash inside a gift bag. Then she went back later to retrieve it and it was gone. This was captured by CCTV footage.

By the time of the trial, Hunter had been sober for five years. He had married Melissa Cohen, an American citizen from South Africa who he met in Los Angeles. They quickly fell in love. She was extremely supportive of Hunter and helped him build a new life. She saw in him the goodness and light that I knew he possessed. Together they had a child they named Beau, who looked eerily like his namesake. Hunter had written a successful memoir, *Beautiful Things*, which discussed his journey as an addict. He also began creating gorgeous paintings that I hung in the residence and in my White House office.

So much had changed for Hunter. He'd committed to his sobriety and truly turned his life around. He had a new wife and new baby, he'd reconnected with his daughters, and he'd found work making the world a better place, eventually becoming development director for a homelessness nonprofit in Los Angeles.

And yet I was taken right back to those chaotic days when the prosecution played a clip of Hunter reading his own audiobook. I had read Hunter's book when it came out. It was painful to be made aware of the details of his life in those years, but I was also impressed with Hunter for being so honest, and for having gotten sober. Still, hearing his voice read the part of the audiobook about his cross-country odyssey in 2017 was very emotional. I had to work to hold it together. The life he described was so desperate.

Before that book, which came out two and a half months into Joe's administration, few people in the family spoke about Hunter's "addiction." Everyone spoke about him not being well, or something being wrong with him, but it was never "Hunter's an addict. Hunter needs help." It was the book that taught us how to stare the ugliness of addiction in the face, to name it, to do whatever we could to support his sobriety.

The prosecution played the audiobook clip, I supposed, to illustrate the depravity of Hunter's existence leading up to the gun purchase in 2018, and to shock everyone with how many hundreds of thousands of dollars he'd spent on drugs.

In the section they shared, Hunter was on the road, strung out, and he got lost driving through the California desert. An owl flew overhead—he felt it was there to guide his car—and he followed the owl to where he needed to be.

Beau, I thought. Whether the owl was real or a hallucination, I believed that the spirit of Beau was at work in trying to help guide his brother to safety. Next to me, Ashley began sobbing. I put my arm around her and hugged her. As I did, I saw the press staring at us and taking notes.

They were looking for any emotion, any sign that the strain was getting to us as we squeezed together on the benches, freezing. I concentrated on not showing any emotion at all, and I tried coaching Ashley and Melissa, who were on either side of me, to stay calm, too, but they didn't always listen. They were especially rattled by the presence of the person who'd published the contents of Hunter's lost laptop, as well as Ashley's therapy journal.

So I understood the impulse when Melissa lost her temper at the man who seemed hell-bent on tormenting our family. She screamed at him in the hallway, a moment that would wind up all over the news. I took her arm and I whispered, "Don't give them that, Melissa."

On a break, I headed toward the restroom to compose myself, but the different sides were being kept apart, so I had to wait to go that way down the hallway. I asked if it would be okay to duck into a stairwell to get a moment by myself.

"I just need a minute," I said.

In the stairwell, I leaned against the gritty concrete wall and took deep breaths. On the other side of the door was a cacophony of reporters, lawyers, and onlookers. After a minute in the quiet with my eyes closed, I reluctantly opened the door and returned to the loud hallway, then to the ice-cold courtroom.

Once the trial was over for the day, I went to the airport, where I took the thirty-minute flight back to DC for the Congressional picnic. At the White House, I changed into a white floral dress. After being briefed in the Diplomatic Reception Room, I stepped out onto the South Portico to give my remarks. Standing there, I looked out at the South Lawn at about a thousand guests, including more than two hundred members of Congress, and smiled. I gave a short speech introducing Joe, who then took to the lectern. We worked the rope line, and then I flew back to Delaware, arriving home after nine p.m.

June 5

This day in court, the prosecution kept the narrative going about Hunter's prolific drug use. His former wife, Kathleen, mother of three of my granddaughters, testified about having found crack pipes in 2015. She spoke plainly about having encouraged him to go to rehab. A woman I'd never seen before, and who was identified as a girlfriend of Hunter's from 2018, testified that she took his money and credit cards, stayed with him at various hotels, and got him drugs. They granted her immunity for testifying.

I'm not one for conspiracy theories, but I was sitting there thinking, *Do drug users often get their fellow drug users to pose with drugs?* She had taken well-framed, well-lit pictures of the drug scale, of the drugs, of her and Hunter together with the drugs, almost as if she were filming a nature documentary.

Around four that afternoon, I headed to the airport to fly to Paris to meet Joe for official business. On the flight across the ocean, I picked at my chicken marsala and felt sorry that I'd be missing Beau's widow, Hallie, testifying the next day. Hallie's mother had recently died, and she wouldn't have her own mother there to lean on.

At least Hallie would have her new husband, John, by her side. Just days before the trial, Hallie got married in Ohio. I couldn't bring myself to attend, but I went over to say goodbye before they left for the wedding weekend. She and John were excited to start their new life together, and he seemed to be a good match for her.

I was happy for them, but I found it overwhelming to see her starting a new life with someone else. In my mind, she would always be Beau's wife, no matter her new marriage or what had occurred with Hunter. I couldn't bear to be reminded in such a powerful way that Beau really was gone forever.

In a way, the dynamic was déjà vu. When I married Joe in 1977, Neilia had been deceased for five years. I wondered then about the impact of Joe's remarriage on Neilia's parents, the Hunters, but I could never have known their pain. They were kind and gracious toward me when I saw them a few times a year when I picked up the boys after their visits. Since Hallie's remarriage, my grandchildren have acquired a new set of grandparents with whom to share holidays and birthdays and special trips. John's family has embraced my grandchildren with an abundance of love.

June 6

A year earlier, by coincidence, I'd been in France when I found out that Hunter's plea deal had fallen apart. In July 2023, Ashley and I were touring Mont Saint-Michel to celebrate the US rejoining UNESCO after the former president had pulled us out. As I'd understood it, lying on a gun-purchase form was the kind of charge that was nearly always pleaded down. But it seemed that someone wanted to make an example of Hunter, and Joe was not about to step in to use his influence to protect him.

On that day in 2023, with the First Lady of France, Brigitte Macron, and the press surrounding me, and one of the wonders of the world before my eyes, I couldn't let on how crushed I was. In the months that followed, somehow I didn't believe that an offense of so little consequence would really go to trial. But it did.

Now, a year later, mid-trial, I arrived in Paris at six in the morning, facing a full day of state business. I showered at an airport lounge, and as I was doing my hair and makeup, someone brought in a tray of the flakiest almond croissants I'd ever tasted. I loved French pastries, and yet I wouldn't sample much on that trip. To make it back for the next day of the trial, I wouldn't sleep a single night in France. The top of my schedule that day read:

> **Paris, France → Carpiquet, France → Colleville-sur-Mer, France → Saint-Laurent-sur-Mer, France → Carpiquet, France → Orly, France → Wilmington, DE**

By ten a.m., Joe and I were at the Normandy American Cemetery landing zone to celebrate the World War II D-Day American veterans on the eightieth anniversary of the invasion. Steven Spielberg, JPMorgan Chase CEO Jamie Dimon, General Mark Milley, presidential biographer Jon Meacham, and Tom Hanks were there, too, as were several dozen members of Congress and their guests. The veterans' average age was 101, but they were in good spirits, and so many warmly told Joe they supported him. Joe gave an excellent speech. Straight from there, we put on mics and went to do an interview with David Muir of ABC News.

I think every single American feels moved by the site of Normandy Beach and the thought of how much those service members endured. Being there made me think of my father, who'd fought in World War II, and of Beau, who'd served many years later in Iraq.

After our time with the military heroes, we met with Brigitte and Emmanuel Macron. We greeted one another as old friends against the backdrop of Omaha Beach. Then we attended the D-Day Anniversary Commemoration Ceremony along with more than twelve thousand guests. This international ceremony was longer than expected, about an hour and a half, but I loved the flyovers—all seven of them.

As the day wound down, we bid farewell to the Macrons, and I headed back to the airport to return to Delaware.

June 7

Back in Wilmington, watching the gun-store employee testify, I found myself confused. Why didn't the judge allow certain things for evidence that pointed to inconsistencies in the store's account of the form's completion and the background check? I sat there mystified but kept quiet, willing myself to appear as much like a robot as possible.

But as my granddaughter Naomi took the stand, I felt anxiety flood my body. As a lawyer, she was not unfamiliar with court proceedings. Still, as a daughter, she had a vested interest in not hurting her father's case if she could help it.

The lawyers asked if Hunter was doing drugs the month he bought the revolver. She said she didn't remember.

"Have you ever done drugs?" they asked her.

What kind of a question is that to ask a young pregnant woman whose father is on trial? I thought.

She described introducing Peter, her boyfriend (by the time of the trial, he was her husband), to her father in 2018, and how she was proud of her dad for having gotten sober. She said he was much the same on another visit to New York that year.

Then the prosecution surprised her with texts she and her father had exchanged on the New York trip. His texts, sent in the middle of the night, seemed confusing. She seemed rattled, and as she left the courtroom, she gave her father a kiss goodbye and then wept on the way out. From where I sat, I could see her hands shaking.

In the anteroom afterward, Hunter cried recalling the way the prosecution badgered Naomi. I tried to comfort him.

"Yes, it's so hard to see your children attacked," I said. "I should know."

Hunter's lawyers said they'd take the weekend to decide if Hunter should testify, too. In the meantime, I had to return to my duties as First Lady. I took a 4:30 p.m. flight back to France.

June 8

For the second time that week, I landed in Paris at dawn. I was whisked to the InterContinental Paris Le Grand. The first part of the day's arrival ceremony was at the Arc de Triomphe to lay a wreath at the Tomb of the Unknown Soldier before the Macrons and close to a thousand invited guests.

From there, I traveled with Brigitte in the Champs-Élysées parade procession to the palace, where we did a series of meet-and-greets in the courtyard and then a gift exchange in the Salon des Portraits. Brigitte and I got to have lunch alone. We discussed how tough politics is on our children and grandchildren. She mentioned that conservative US commentator Candace Owens made false claims that Brigitte was born male and transitioned. Brigitte was right—anyone can say anything about you, and you have little recourse unless you sue. (The Macrons did sue in July 2025—and won, offering medical records and photos of Brigitte pregnant, to prove that Owens's claims were ridiculous.) Then there was a meeting with Bernard Arnault and Suzanne Pagé, with whom we saw the Matisse and Ellsworth Kelly exhibits at the Louis Vuitton Foundation.

I had about an hour to change into my gown—a blue velvet Schiaparelli that I was relieved to find fit in spite of the quick turnaround for alterations—before the dinner. At the cocktail reception, I greeted dozens of French and American celebrities. The Macrons had done an amazing job with the lavish state dinner for 230 guests.

I crawled into bed back at the InterContinental around eleven at night.

June 9

Paris, France → Orly, France → Château-Thierry, France → Belleau, France → Château-Thierry, France → Orly, France → Philadelphia, PA → Wilmington, DE

Before we left France, we did photo lines at the hotel, attended a reception to greet the US embassy staff, then flew to the Aisne-Marne American Cemetery to honor the fallen of World War I. I was home in Delaware at about eight that night, ready to learn how Hunter's trial would conclude.

June 10

Hunter's lawyer did a solid wrap-up, and then it was time to await the verdict. We didn't know how long it would take, but we thought it might be hours or even days. Once the jury withdrew to deliberate, I drove home, about fifteen minutes away, and stayed close to my phone awaiting news. Hunter and Melissa stayed a bit closer, at the Hotel Du Pont just down the street from the courthouse. About an hour later, we were told that the jury had suspended deliberations and gone home. They'd return the following day.

June 11

The next morning, not long after they reconvened, we were told that the jury had already reached a decision. My sister Bonny and I raced back to the courthouse in the car, but we just missed the reading of the verdict.

As we got off the elevator and turned the corner, Hunter and his lawyer were already walking out of the courtroom. We went with them into a little holding room right off the court. The family and the lawyers were there, and it was evident that it had not gone well. Many of them were crying, but Hunt was amazing. He was strong, and he praised his lawyer for doing a good job.

The lawyer appeared stunned that he had not won because he'd almost never lost a case. We hadn't expected Hunter to be found guilty on all three counts either. I called Naomi afterward to give her the news. She answered but was so upset she couldn't speak. It broke my heart.

I knew I had to be strong for her, to tell her how composed her dad had been for everyone after the verdict. He spoke calmly and gratefully about how even though he'd lost the case, he felt he'd won because so many people had supported him. I told Naomi that she was one of the people who'd been there, that she'd done a good job.

It was hard for me not to think about the role politics played in the matter going to trial in the first place. Attorney General Merrick Garland oversaw the Justice Department in its handling of Hunter's case. In the end, it felt like in working so hard to be impartial, we guaranteed that Hunter would meet the worst possible legal fate. Joe might have gone too far, in my opinion, to show that his family was being treated with complete impartiality.

At the beach house after the verdict, I stood in my kitchen and thought about an encounter at the White House Correspondents' Association (WHCA) dinner the prior year. The hardships of others going through more serious crises than mine helped me put my own grief into perspective.

A couple named Ella Milman and Mikhail Gershkovich, the parents of Evan Gershkovich, had come through the receiving line. I'd seen in my briefing book that they'd be attending. Evan was a *Wall Street Journal* reporter wrongly imprisoned in Russia on fake spy charges. I wondered what it must be like to have your son falsely imprisoned in another country. When their names were read, I saw them rush up to Joe, their eyes questioning.

Joe called over to have Secretary of State Antony Blinken join them.

Ella said that a promised letter on Evan's behalf hadn't been sent. Joe told Antony to make sure it got out. I stepped back from the group, feeling that I was invading a private moment in which they wanted to talk to Joe.

As they moved on, I said to Joe, "God, how do they do it? It must be so hard."

At the WHCA dinner, a plea was made by the journalists to get Evan free, and Joe promised he wouldn't give up—and he didn't. Evan was one of the hostages Joe would help free mere months later.

I walked into the kitchen from the back porch, musing about how tenacious Ella had been about her son's release—never giving up, always pushing, pushing, pushing.

At that moment, I happened to look out the window. Standing at the back window of her house was my neighbor, another mother gazing out on the day. Her son had died three years earlier at the age of fifteen. The grief she must have experienced, the ache that never goes away. I thought of what Tupac's mother, Afeni Shakur, said after her son was murdered in a drive-by shooting: "I don't want you to think your heart is gonna heal. If someone told you that, they told you an untruth."

Mothers and sons. A complicated relationship I knew well. So much joy and so much pain. So many layers to break down, to rebuild, so much work to tamp down the hurt. To me, the mother-and-son bond might be the strongest connection on earth. Certainly it brought out my protectiveness more than anything else. I was so glad I'd been there for Hunter and also not let my other responsibilities slip.

More than anything, I was glad that what was at once one of the most excruciating and most meaningful weeks of my life was finally over.

CHAPTER 28

In February 2024, I hit the campaign trail for Joe for what I thought might be the last time in my life. I resolved to leave it all out on the field, and I was thrilled to see how many politicians and celebrities were joining me in the effort to get Joe reelected. Traveling all over the country, I shared this basic message:

> We know what the Republican playbook is—they are going to paint Joe as too old and not up for the job. They're going to repeat it and repeat it and repeat it. Just like they did with the 2020 election results. But we don't have to be complicit in their big lie. You know Joe. He's been to your homes; you've had long discussions with him; you've seen him in action. You all know that yes, he's eighty-one. But you also know that at eighty-one, he does more in an hour than most people do in a day.
>
> In addition to that, he has wisdom, strength, empathy, and vision. He has delivered on so many of his promises as president precisely because he's learned a lot in those eighty-one years. His age, with his experience and expertise, is an incredible asset, and he proves it every day. Look at all he's

> accomplished: He rescued our country from the depths of a pandemic. He vaccinated an entire nation. He delivered one of the strongest economic recoveries in modern history. He created fourteen million jobs. Gas prices are down. Inflation is down. Energy costs are down. He got bipartisan legislation passed—even in the midst of this hyper-partisan environment.
>
> No other president could do all that; only Joe—yes, with his eighty-one years of experience and expertise—could have done all that and more. We can take nothing for granted. Our fundamental rights are at stake. Our democracy is at risk. Our basic humanity as a country is on the line. We don't want to wake up like we did in 2016—and say, "Oh my God, what just happened?"

I wasn't unaware of what Americans were feeling. Prices were still too high. Joe knew that. But the alternative would be far worse. Throughout our time in Washington, I'd seen how out of touch many politicians were.

Early in Joe's career, a member of the Washington elite came and sat in our living room, full of the kids' toys and our newspapers and whatever else, and he looked horrified by the casualness. He said to me, in all seriousness, "Wow, I never saw *paperbacks* on a bookshelf." That was the kind of snobbery of those days. I told Joe what he said and we both laughed about it. Nevertheless, we moved the paperbacks out of that room so we wouldn't offend any of Joe's other colleagues' sensibilities.

The age question was there, but it seemed that every time people had doubts about his abilities, he would do something that would reassure people he was still sharp. At his State of the Union address on March 7, Republican lawmakers and a guest in the gallery heckled him. Joe not only stayed calm and kept going with his excellent speech, but he also responded swiftly and effectively to the taunts, using them as an opportunity to push more vigorously for his policy agenda.

Also that month, *Vogue* editor in chief Anna Wintour brilliantly organized the historic, three-thousand-person "Three Presidents" event at Radio City Music Hall. Anna's idea was for Joe to rise from the floor on a platform with Barack Obama and Bill Clinton. However, some feared that the rising platform would be courting the nickname "Broadway Joe." My feeling: Anna was always right about that sort of thing; regardless, it was her event, so she shouldn't be second-guessed.

Her vision prevailed. It was moving watching the presidents rise into view together, all three of them looking happy and relaxed, such a contrast to the rallies of Joe's lone, angry opponent. The entertainment that night was amazing. Lizzo was incredible, and Stephen Colbert did a great job leading a conversation in which Bill and Barack talked about how much good Joe had done.

The campaign this time was headquartered in Wilmington, not Philadelphia as before. This was a real source of pride among Wilmingtonians, and Joe and I were so grateful for the warm welcome they gave our staff. Young, bright minds and energy arrived from all across the country to work on the campaign. Julie Chávez Rodriguez, Quentin Fulks, Rob Flaherty, and Jen O'Malley Dillon built an incredible team.

Growing up, I was a huge Barbra Streisand fan. I even went to one of her farewell concerts. Cut to the present day: There I was, on the phone with her, asking her to join an event for Joe that summer. When I first called, she was asleep. When I called later from the beach in Rehoboth, she apologized for missing the call.

"Honey, I stay up until two or three in the morning and then sleep in," she said.

Had Barbra Streisand—Babs herself—just called me "honey"? I'd met the queen of England, most of the leaders of the free world, and countless movie stars. But that was the starriest thing that had ever happened to me.

"No, no, don't apologize!" I said. "I'm sorry I called in the morning. I do the opposite. I'm an early riser." I told her I hoped she would come to LA to show her support for Joe at the fundraiser.

"I can't write a speech," she said.

I was sympathetic. Public speaking can be scary no matter how often you're onstage. My staff went through a phase of sending me speech revisions up until the last second, to the point where sometimes I was given only minutes to rehearse before jumping onstage. Exasperated one day by the expectation that I perform well under those circumstances, I made a sign in Sharpie and posted it on the wall: I AM NOT A ROBOT.

"I'll have it done for you," I told Barbra.

"Well, how long?" she asked.

"Five to seven minutes?"

"No, too long."

"How about three?"

"Okay—I'm so upset about what's happening in the world right now," she said. "All I want to do is drive around in my truck with my husband."

Can you imagine pulling up next to Barbra in her truck at a stoplight?

"I'll be wearing a big dress and flat shoes," she said.

"Perfect," I said.

When I was in eighth grade, I became obsessed with her album *My Name Is Barbra*. How many times did my friend Susan's sister play that album? Over and over again. Now here we were—she, eighty-two; me, seventy-three—talking about flats versus heels. How strange life is sometimes.

At the event, I was, of course, thrilled to see her. She gave me a big hug and did a terrific job with her three-minute speech.

Joe seemed tired—overly tired. He was pushing too hard, traveling too much. Inside a couple of weeks, he'd done two round trips to Europe—for D-Day in France, back to Delaware, then to the G7 in Italy—and gone out to Los Angeles, then Delaware again, before heading to Camp David for debate prep.

I'd been on the road for a few weeks—at the launch of Seniors for Biden; doing talks in Wisconsin, Minnesota, California, and Arizona; then meeting with Women for Biden. In addition to campaigning for Joe, I was teaching and had my First Lady tasks—sampling salmon entrées for a forthcoming NATO dinner, ordering the Christmas decorations, hosting Pride at the White House. While Joe was preparing for the debate, I hit the trail again to keep the momentum going.

Carole King was scheduled to perform at a fundraiser held in a private home in Philadelphia's Chestnut Hill neighborhood on June 24. On that evening, she said she hadn't been feeling well, and so while she'd be happy to perform, she wasn't sure she'd be up to doing more than one song. I said that would be plenty; it would just be amazing to have her there. Dozens of people were crowded into the house, standing on steps all the way up the staircase to listen to her sing.

"I love coming to Philadelphia for events because you're the only ones who understand my accent," I said. I told a brief account of the story of our life, and I said Joe was "the strong, steady one, always unflappable, always unflinching through highs and lows of our country and this world—a pandemic, an assault on the Capitol, war. He is that same steady leader. The faithful warrior battling for the soul of this nation." I contrasted that with Joe's opponent and the terrible things he'd said about veterans—calling John McCain "a loser" and "not a war hero" because he had been captured.

Finally, I said, "I know what's on your mind, so let's talk about age and this election. This election's not about age. Joe and the other guy are about the same age. This election is about character, wisdom, and ability."

I then introduced Carole, who did one song and then just kept going, singing "Up on the Roof," "You've Got a Friend," and "Where You Lead." Looking around the room, it felt like we were all having a moment together—of joy, hope, and determination that we would not let chaos return to power.

The first presidential debate was set for June 27 in Atlanta, Georgia, to be hosted by CNN. Joe was at debate camp from June 20 to June 27. Essentially, that's where the candidate is prepped daily by advisors and speechwriters. Mock debates are held to prepare for various attacks or opportunities that might arise. Sometimes the debate-prep team will even build a version of the set where the debate will be held and adjust everything to match it, from the lighting to the temperature, so when the candidate gets out onstage, surprises are kept to a minimum. Joe and I talked every night. He seemed off to me. But, always the optimist, Joe said he felt that things were going well.

On the day of the debate, I finished a campaign stop at Virginia

Beach and headed to Atlanta. Hotels on the trail are disorienting, because you get off the plane, the Secret Service puts you into a car, and you're whisked to the location. You're never led through the elegant, marble-floored lobby. For safety, you pull into an underground parking garage and are shuttled along a service-entrance path that inevitably wends right by garbage cans reeking of rotting room service leftovers mixed with discarded mini shampoos—an odor so sour and pungent that it almost knocks you down.

Typically, you're ushered through an industrial kitchen, its floors alternately sticky and slippery. Often, by the time you get through the underground maze to your room, you have no idea what hotel you're at, what floor you're on, what city you're in. After such a journey, I arrived at the hotel suite where Joe was staying.

When I got to the suite, I saw the usual buffet laid out on the counter—always ridiculous amounts of food—and the TV turned to a news channel. I saw his aides Annie Tomasini and Jacob Spreyer, and I asked them where Joe was. Jacob said he was taking a nap, and he pointed to one of the bedrooms. I walked in and Joe looked bleary. He had just woken up.

"Joe," I said, "you've got to get ready. Makeup's coming in."

"I don't feel well," he said. His voice sounded raspy.

"What's the matter?" I asked.

He said, "I don't know. I just don't feel well."

Joe had often been sick or exhausted going into a major event, but he was instantly cured when he walked out on a stage. I've heard actors refer to this as "Dr. Footlights." I've seen it again and again with Joe and public events.

"Well, I'm just going to leave you alone to take your shower and get dressed," I said.

Jacob went in and briefed him a little bit while he was getting dressed. The amazing makeup artist Tim Quinn came in and did Joe's makeup. Then it was time to head to the arena.

In the elevator, I looked over at Joe, and I did a double take. He looked like he was made of clay, strangely monochromatic. My first thought was that Tim had made a rare mistake.

But no, it wasn't Tim's fault. There was just something very wrong. I had to quiet my own mind. I reassured myself: *He always rallies. He responds to the energy of the moment. He'll do fine.* He'd done something like fifteen major debates by then. No matter how awful he felt, he would get up there and he would deliver.

We got off the elevator. I gave Joe a hug and a kiss. I was confident that in spite of not feeling his best, he would do well. Joe took a right and headed into a room with some of his senior advisors. I went straight into another holding room to watch the debate with Anthony Bernal, with Annie occasionally coming in and out.

The debate began. In the audience were only the moderators, Dana Bash and Jake Tapper, at a table at the foot of the stage. I immediately noticed that Joe didn't look good. He didn't seem himself from the opening. It was almost like with every line his energy dropped and he had to regroup. I wasn't listening to the words. I was looking at the body language. He kept putting his head down. I said out loud to the television, "Pick your head up! Look into the camera!"

I was imagining what it would be like to be watching as one of my sisters, or as one of the women I'd met that day in Virginia Beach. How would they be perceiving Joe? I could see myself having the debate on while I cleaned up my kitchen, graded papers, or folded the laundry. Half-watching, I would still be able to tell that he was struggling.

"Give me the numbers! Be specific," he was surely saying that whole debate-prep time—he always wanted to be precise when he made points about policy, and to offer exact statistics. When he asked me for advice, I told him, "Talk from the heart. Tell people you know prices are too high at the grocery store and say what you're doing to fix it. Don't just talk about inflation percentages. It's about how you make people *feel*."

When I speak at events, I can tell that a lot of people are not necessarily taking in all the words, but they're looking at my shoes, or the pin on my blazer, or my posture. The general impression you make counts for so much in politics. I imagined that even with the sound off, no one could think the debate was going well for Joe.

A few minutes in, Anthony gasped. Joe had said something nonsensical about beating Medicare. *Is he short-circuiting?* I thought. *Is this a stroke?* It felt like we were watching an AI hologram of the man we knew, and the hologram was glitching. *Has he been drugged? Oh God—will people watching assume that this is how he is all the time?*

Our holding room was dead silent. Anthony and I had known each other so long we didn't have to speak to know what the other was thinking. In that debate, Joe lost himself. He lost the essence of who he was. He did not speak from the heart. His opponent lied more than a hundred times, but that didn't matter.

My first guess was that he'd just frozen. He'd choked. In competitive sports, there's a phenomenon known as "overtraining syndrome," a term I heard when swimmer Simone Manuel, Katie Ledecky's former teammate, failed to qualify for the Tokyo Olympics. Perhaps Joe had been overcoached?

As the debate went on, my mind was racing. I was waiting for Joe to punch back, but he looked lost. What was going on? Was he having a medical emergency?

While that Medicare moment was a low point, the whole debate was awkward. He couldn't get into a rhythm. The night was unprecedented. Even if he stumbled in the course of a public event—and his whole life, his childhood stutter came out when he was tired—he'd eventually get into a groove. Joe did improve in the course of that debate, but not enough to reassure me or anyone watching that he was okay. He clearly wasn't. So what was wrong? Nothing explained what I was seeing. I'd never seen that look on his face before in my life.

Finally, someone came into the room and said to me, "He has five minutes left, if you want to go out."

As soon as the debate ended, I walked out onto the stage. Our eyes locked. He smiled at me and we hugged.

Up close, Joe looked weary, but he seemed more like himself than he had even fifteen minutes earlier.

His opponent walked off the stage.

"Let's go say hello to Jake and Dana," Joe said.

I didn't want to go say hi to anyone. But at every debate Joe liked to personally greet the moderators.

I looked over to where they were sitting and saw that the floor was covered in stripes. I couldn't tell if the stripes were steps or not. I had heels on, so I said, "Let me take a hold of your arm, Joe."

This image would be taken as evidence that he needed to lean on *me* for support and that I had to lead him. Have you seen my shoes? I am a "the higher the heel, the closer to God" woman. Joe was never leaning on me, I promise.

We went down to say hello and goodbye to the moderators, and they were almost completely silent. I thought, *Wow, this really has gone terribly.*

Then it was officially over. As we walked off the stage, Joe whispered to me, "I really f**ked up, didn't I?"

"Yes, you did," I whispered back.

To this day, I still don't know what happened. Why wasn't he making any sense? It was inexplicable to me. The only other time he'd sounded like that was right after he'd had surgery. I wish I'd thought of asking for a blood test, just so we'd know what was in his system. Had he taken something on the plane for his cough, something at the hotel to sleep—codeine cough syrup or Ambien? I'd been on the campaign trail and hadn't been with him, so I had no idea. I only wish I had the answer.

In politics, bad nights happen. I thought back to the New Hampshire primary, when we left for South Carolina. On nights like that, there is no time to stop and reflect. You have to keep moving. In the car from the arena to the hotel where Joe was set to do the first of three postdebate events, Annie broke the silence. "Hundreds of people are waiting at the hotel for you to address them," she said. "Shoulders back. Smile."

Joe looked grim. The fact that he knew it was bad I took as a sign of his having returned to himself. As we made our way from the car to the backstage area, the staff that was moving with us—always, there are at least thirty or forty people in the presidential entourage, from the person with the nuclear football to the doctor to the advance people to the Secret Service—looked like they had just been gut-punched. Nobody knew what to say.

The crowd was still energetic and enthusiastic. Many of them had been campaigning during the day and were now unwinding with some drinks. The DJ was keeping the energy high. I went up onstage to introduce Joe. Anthony reminded me, "Be positive! High energy! The crowd is fired up. Oh, and *smile*!"

I grimaced—I was always the one telling everyone else to smile more.

As a teacher, I believe in leading with praise no matter how bad the test result or essay is. So I became my teacher self onstage. I couldn't say, "Wasn't that a great debate, everyone?" Because it wasn't, and that would be phony. But I knew Joe was hurt and had to hear something positive. I was trying to move forward and stay upbeat. So I got up there next to Joe and, with a smile on my face, I said, honestly, "You answered every question. You knew all the facts. And let me ask the crowd: What did Trump do? Lie."

Indeed, Joe's opponent had dodged any question he hadn't wanted to answer. Joe had tried to give full answers to every question. But looking back, my comments probably sounded a little too disconnected from what people saw. I wonder if, from those very first moments after the debate, we were trying so hard to reassure everyone that we didn't take the time to acknowledge that he looked very unwell in that debate, to say to the public: "Yes. That was bad, no doubt."

Maybe only then, once we validated people's disquiet, could we continue the conversation and find an explanation. The truth was, Joe was not who he was on a day-to-day basis in that debate. At the event with supporters that followed, his energy returned; he recovered his rhythm. As the crowd cheered Joe in that hotel ballroom, he revived. Not an hour after the debate, he spoke well. I found the speech eloquent, even beautiful. Still, the staff remained in shock; you could read it on their faces. Somehow we still had two more stops to make that night.

After the hotel event, we were whisked back into the car and driven to Waffle House. This is the kind of postdebate activity that gets planned when you think the debate will go well—a victory lap through town, some pancakes at midnight. When we walked into the restaurant, we saw that the place was packed. Part of the crowd was thrilled to see Joe. A group of young people looked up from their breakfast platters and cheered when they saw him. Many people wanted selfies and hugs. Joe and I were both having our hands shaken again and again by palms sticky with maple syrup.

But part of the restaurant was looking at us with blunt hostility. There were far more MAGA supporters there than we had anticipated. Meanwhile, news reports were coming in on our phones, and none of it was making us feel any better. This was when we first began to hear the chatter about how, clearly, Joe's cognitive decline must have been concealed deliberately by those around him so we could stay in power.

To me, it was so absurd that I couldn't imagine ever having to dignify it with a response. I never guessed that theory would take on a life of its own.

Finally, Joe and I took our order to go from Waffle House and made our way to the airport to fly to our final stop of the night: Raleigh, North Carolina.

We landed around two in the morning. Amazingly, given the hour, a substantial crowd of smiling people had gathered, and they even had a band there playing music. I walked off the plane and out onto the tarmac feeling dizzy. The night was pitch-black, but the area by the plane was lit with spotlights.

"Great debate!" someone actually said, shaking Joe's hand.

We felt enduring enthusiasm for Joe's candidacy. There were still a lot of believers. Joe was fine on the flight. And yet, I was distraught. I tried to be cheerful for the crowds, who, after all, had trekked out to an airfield in the middle of the night just to wish us well.

On the Raleigh tarmac, Joe and I smiled and shook hands in that odd oasis of light until it was time, at last, to go to bed. We were driven to a hotel, and for a few hours, we were able to sleep before facing the aftermath.

The next morning, I woke up first as usual. After I had my coffee, I went in to wake Joe up. There was a heaviness. I said, "Get up. We're not going to let ninety minutes define a whole career."

That day, he gave what I thought of as one of his all-time best speeches. He spoke from the heart:

"Folks, I don't walk as easy as I used to, I don't speak as smoothly as I used to. I don't debate as well as I used to, but . . . I know how to tell the truth. I know right from wrong, and I know how to do this job. I know, like millions of Americans know, when you get knocked down, you get back up."

Standing by him in my VOTE VOTE VOTE dress designed by Christian Siriano, I felt that we were moving forward. But that feeling didn't last. The biggest lesson for us, I think, was that if you don't explain something well enough then the question won't go away. There was never a satisfying enough explanation offered for Joe's debate performance, and a lot of people never got over it. Everywhere we went, we still heard people shouting, "Stick with it!" and "You've got this!" But from that moment on, there was also a drumbeat calling on him to get out of the race. In the days to come, it would grow louder and louder.

CHAPTER 29

Every morning in the following weeks, before I was fully awake, I had the feeling that something awful had happened. As I opened my eyes and sat up, I remembered what it was—the debate. Joe's performance had scared people into believing that he was suffering from a profound cognitive decline and that he wasn't mentally fit to be president.

To me, and to those who spent the most time with him, the man on that stage was not who we saw on a daily basis. Yes, he was older. He seemed tired more often. But Joe's closest advisors said the campaign remained viable, and they insisted that Joe owed it to the country to stay in the race.

Over the years, there had been uncomfortable moments, to be sure. I flinched when Joe said, at the White House press conference after the Hur Report was released, "The president of Mexico, Sisi, did not want to open up the gate to allow humanitarian material to get in." He meant "the president of Egypt." The truth was that he was not performing as well as he had in his younger days. Did that disqualify him from being president, as long as he was still getting the job done? I didn't think so, nor did the staff members who were spending far more time with him than I was.

The optimistic thinking was that enough voters would say, "Okay, he's old, but he's been doing a good job. There's a young vice president. If during his second term he gets to the point where he needs to hand over power, the worst-case scenario would still be good."

If you knew Joe Biden well, you'd know that if he actually got to the point where he wasn't capable of doing the job, he would step down. Certainly, if he exhibited cognitive impairment, I would not hesitate to say so. His staff would not hesitate to say so. But he was nowhere near that point in the summer of 2024.

While I'd never cared for politics, I'd been around it long enough to become pragmatic about elections. Campaigning in New Hampshire during the 2020 primary, I'd gotten in trouble for bluntly saying, "Your candidate might be better on, I don't know, health care than Joe is, but you've got to look at who's going to win this election, and maybe you have to swallow a little bit and say, 'Okay, I personally like so-and-so better, but your bottom line has to be that we have to beat Trump.'"

"*Swallow*?" an aide of mine teased after that event. "What's next, Jill—'suck it up'?"

Note taken. But in July 2024, even after the debate, based on what I was seeing, I believed Joe was the best bet for preventing the return of an administration that seemed likely to bring chaos. I felt that even if people thought a younger candidate would be more exciting to people, it made sense for the party to stay with Joe. He was the incumbent, a huge advantage. Plus, he'd done so much good. He had integrity. People who spent as much time around him as I did were not nearly as worried as Democratic elites seemed to be.

But alarming information kept trickling in. I was told that people had begun telling fundraisers to stop giving to Joe's campaign. Someone I barely knew texted me to say it looked like "time to take the car keys away from Grandpa." I found that so presumptuous and so condescending—and it was one of what felt like hourly calls for him to step aside. It began to feel like death by a thousand paper cuts.

Was there anyone else who could beat Trump? A year earlier, the best Democratic minds hadn't thought so when they implored him to run. Now what?

As long as there was still a campaign in front of us, I stayed on the trail to reach as many people as possible each day. Time is the only commodity that isn't replenishable on a campaign. On the road, warm crowds were coming out for Joe. I saw the enthusiasm.

There was chatter around the concept of Joe taking a cognitive test. My belief was that it would not be a challenge for him. Why not give people that test score so they felt assured of his competency? I said as much to Joe, but I was at odds with his advisors. They argued to him that every day on the job was a cognitive test, and that it was absurd for people to think that an ability to count backward by threes or whatever the test required would satisfy anyone if his track record didn't.

Our first real sign that major forces were rallying to ease Joe out of the race was a call from Barack raising the issue.

If I stepped outside my role as the protective spouse, I understood Barack's point of view. Barack had been the change candidate. He'd been leading the Democrats into a new era, a new party. Joe had been in the government for decades; he was never going to be a change candidate. Still, overhearing Joe on that phone call, I felt flat. If I'd been asked what would be best for the family, I knew the answer was clear: Get out. The price of entry into politics is being judged incessantly. No one gives you leeway or grace. You're looked at with a skeptical eye—

the way you speak, any misstep. But I wanted whatever was best for the country. Ultimately, this was Joe's decision and his alone.

Which polls, which advisors, which news stories could Joe trust? When it came to his health, the doctors would know best, wouldn't they? His doctor said he had passed his annual checkup with flying colors in February. Every year, he met with a cardiologist, a neurologist, a dermatologist—just like all his predecessors. His doctors told Joe that there was no need for testing beyond this extensive battery, and no reason to do a cognitive test.

It was decided that the fear had to be quelled by Joe and Joe alone. He began to get out there and fight harder for himself. In an ABC News interview on July 5, George Stephanopoulos drilled him on whether he was mentally fit. Joe made the case that the debate was a bad night. He said, "I don't think anybody's more qualified to be president or win this race than me." That interview didn't seem to provide the reassurance people wanted.

On July 10, George Clooney published an essay in *The New York Times*: "I Love Joe Biden. But We Need a New Nominee." He said that the Joe he saw at the fundraiser was the one everyone saw at the debate. "I consider him a friend," Clooney said, "and I believe in him. Believe in his character. Believe in his morals. In the last four years, he's won many of the battles he's faced. But the one battle he cannot win is the fight against time."

Earlier that week, Nancy Pelosi had reached out directly to Joe asking to meet.

I'd first met Nancy in the late 1970s in Rehoboth Beach with her husband, Paul, at the Sussex County Jamboree. After Joe became VP, the relationship deepened. Being around her was natural and easy. When Joe became president, we saw Nancy and Paul even more often—whether at fundraisers or state events—and I became truly fond of them. Joe thought the world of her.

Whenever there was a funeral at the Capitol, she'd be in charge and would greet us, and there she'd be up on those heels, gliding across those hard floors, looking impeccable into her eighties. I admired her elegance and her leadership.

The morning of July 10, Nancy was brought in quietly and ushered into the Yellow Oval at the residence. Joe later told me that she said the question of whether to stay in the race was his decision—but he should drop out. She said Joe would be heartbroken if he heard what the Democrats were saying about him.

That struck a nerve in Joe. He so valued the Congress and had longtime support from members on both sides of the aisle. Earlier that same morning, Nancy Pelosi had gone on *Morning Joe* and said, "It's up to the president to decide if he is going to run. We're all encouraging him to make that decision. Because time is running short . . . He is beloved. He is respected. And people want him to make that decision."

She was asked if she wanted him to run and she said, "I want him to do whatever he decides to do, and that's the way it is. Whatever he decides, we go with."

The next day, Joe did a live press conference at the NATO summit.

On CNN, Van Jones introduced the clip beautifully:

> He's got to walk out there, frankly, on a carpet of prayers. There's a lot of grassroots people who see this very differently than the political professionals like myself. There are a lot of

> African Americans in particular who feel that Donald Trump is getting a free pass. He can say anything, and it's expected that he's going to say crazy stuff, that Joe Biden is being held to a different standard, and it's not fair. And so, there's a lot of prayer out there for Biden that you don't see. There's a lot of people who feel, you know, in the Black community we're so used to seeing leaders stumble and then be attacked. You know, grassroots fundraising is going up for him, phone calls into Black radio stations are going up for him.

I was seeing that support, too—on the trail and in messages coming in from all over. I didn't want to discount the will of the thousands of voters I was interacting with. I didn't want to ignore my own experience of Joe as physically weaker but still mentally fit. I wanted Joe to maintain his dignity and to continue to do the right thing, as he always had. What was the right thing? I hoped it would become clear soon.

Many wanted an open convention. Small whispers turned into a loud roar. To get ahead of this, we had invited Kamala and Doug to join us at the White House Fourth of July celebration that year. It was felt that the visual of all four of us together would signal that this was the ticket, period. If not Joe, then Kamala. We were sticking together.

When people couldn't convince Joe to quit, they began lobbying me. I was encouraged to "be the hero," to come out and say, "I've convinced my husband not to run."

Some people who thought I could be persuaded to tell Joe to drop out insisted that I'd done it before. They pointed to a moment in the lead-up to the 2004 presidential election. But back then, Joe had told me that he didn't want to run that year. Political pundits kept showing up at our house trying to convince him to take on George W. Bush. Day after day, these men in their suits continued to arrive at our home to badger him.

One day, I'd had enough. Sitting by the pool in my bikini, I found myself getting madder and madder. Finally, I wrote "NO" in black Sharpie on my stomach, then walked through their strategy session. I was not saying no to Joe. I was expressing my exasperation with those aggressive men who were tromping through my home trying to make Joe do something he'd explicitly told them he didn't want to do.

In 2016, Joe was contemplating running again. But Beau had just died. I believed that during the campaign, when anything related to Beau came up—the military, cancer, family—Joe would have a raw emotional response. I thought that could be a liability for him. "The people do not want a weeping president," I said. Maybe that wasn't true. People loved it when Bill Clinton felt people's pain and cried. But I'm from an era where it was believed that leaders had to be stoic. Still, if Joe had decided he wanted to run that year, I'd have supported his choice, even if it meant sailing the country on a river of tears.

In 2024, Joe wanted to stay in the race, and so I was going to do my best to support him. Not only did I believe in his ability to do the job, but I also felt inspired by his plans for another term. I believed that he would continue to bring down inflation, protect the environment, fix the tax code, and safeguard women's health. Out on the trail, I felt momentum gathering again behind him.

On July 13, 2024, Joe's opponent was shot at a rally in Pennsylvania by a twenty-year-old man. It was horrifying, and beyond me how it had happened given the usual protocols of locking down an area. The dramatic image of the once and future president with blood on his face, making a fist, was everywhere. I called Melania and said that I was thinking of her and Barron.

She was polite and controlled as ever. She said they were "good," and thanked me for calling.

Out in Las Vegas on July 17, Joe was scheduled to address a large Latino gathering, the UnidosUS Annual Conference. When we spoke that morning, he seemed happy with his speech, but his voice sounded strained. Was he sick again?

A few hours later, I got a call from Annie saying he was coughing a lot.

"Did you COVID test him?" I asked.

"I don't know," she said. "Hold on."

The irony was that throughout the pandemic, every time you sniffled, everyone you'd seen all week got tested. But here, the man clearly had COVID symptoms, and they didn't even think to test him for days? He was positive. Then they had to figure out how to get him home without getting everyone else on the plane sick. They found a way to sequester him on Air Force One, and they flew him back to Delaware Thursday night. At midnight, he arrived at our Rehoboth beach house.

"How's my girl?" Joe asked as he walked into the house, smiling at the staff member sitting up late in the living room. The aide told him that I was already in bed upstairs. That night, Joe slept in a separate bedroom downstairs so he wouldn't get me sick. At least I was trying to sleep; there was a heaviness to those days that led to horrible nightmares about being chased and held down. I wondered how a psychologist would analyze them.

One person after another called to tell Joe what they were seeing: *Your age is a factor. You're underwater. Trump is leading in these polls.*

Joe was obsessed with his iPhone and the Apple News feed, and his algorithm was selecting the worst of the worst. He was constantly watching Fox. He saw and heard all the negative discourse. During campaigns, pollsters become like demigods. This round, it seemed that they all wanted to be in front of the principal with the most dramatic reports.

One thing I heard later was that Joe's inner circle shielded him from bad news and kept him in a bubble of delusional optimism. That's incorrect. He was being deluged with news every day; nearly all of it was bad.

CHAPTER 30

On a rainy Saturday, July 20, 2024, Joe was recovering at our house in Rehoboth Beach but taking national security calls. Later that day, he asked Steve Ricchetti and Mike Donilon to come meet with him on the screened-in porch. While everyone agreed things looked dire, opinions differed as to what to do about it. As many trusted advisors as had been telling Joe to get out, just as many were saying to stay in. One minute you'd have a popular talk show host telling Joe not to give up. Then you'd have a Democratic congressman demanding he drop out immediately. Then you'd have an ambassador saying it might be time to step down. Then numerous world leaders would be insisting, "Stay in! Fight!"

I was conflicted. Above all, I knew the strength of Joe's character, and I was proud of all his administration had accomplished. I felt the people surrounding him were strong, with good judgment. He had a young, capable vice president who could easily have taken the helm if needed. But could we get beyond this?

It had only been about three weeks since the debate, and some felt people would be willing to move past it. Joe still thought things might turn around again and that he could win. After all, he was the incumbent, he had accomplished so much, and there were no candidates polling better. What made staying in impossible was that the Democratic party leaders had already decided he should no longer be the candidate. It felt like at the first flicker of crisis, they splintered and fought and criticized one another. Finally, it was time for Joe to decide if he was going to give in or find some way to endure. There was no playbook for the situation he found himself in.

After Joe spoke for a while to Mike and Steve, he got Hunter on the phone. Hunter insisted there was a pathway to victory. He didn't want his father to drop out. Ashley had said the same thing earlier that week, that the people she worked with kept saying to her, "Tell your dad not to let them paint him a certain way. He's got to keep fighting."

From the porch, Joe called me into the conversation. Once I'd settled myself in a wicker chair, he asked what I thought.

"You have to decide this for yourself," I said. "I cannot decide for you. I don't want you to have my opinion. I will support whatever you choose to do."

Had he grown too old for the job and I hadn't noticed? I didn't think so, but could I be objective enough to be sure? The doctors assured us that he was healthy and able.

At that point, Annie and Anthony were brought into the conversation.

Joe was clear-eyed and steady.

"All right, if we were to do this, how would we do it?" he said.

Mike was asked to go back to his hotel and write up a statement and then return a couple of hours later to talk through it.

Joe had weighed the advice of his most trusted advisors carefully. But I suspected there was one piece of information that influenced him more than the rest. Steve had told him that a group of senators was rumored to be planning to send him a letter telling him that it was time to go.

The Senate had always been the institution that he revered above all others. I always believed that his greatest love was for, in order: God, his family, and then the Senate. Getting that letter might have actually killed him; he'd have died from a broken heart.

Mike drafted the announcement. Together, he and Joe did some tinkering, and then Joe said he was going to sleep on it.

CHAPTER 31

There was little precedent for what was about to happen, and we were just a handful of people in Rehoboth Beach, Delaware. Once it was written, how would the message be sent?

On Sunday, Anthony called Jen O'Malley Dillon, Joe's campaign chair, with a hypothetical question: "What if he had to get a statement out to the world on this topic? How would we do it?"

"Well, we'd have to let Rob know," she said. Rob Flaherty was the deputy campaign manager who oversaw all digital communication for the campaign.

I overheard a conversation about the best time of day to share the news.

"How much daylight do we need?" one asked.

"We should do this at noon," another said.

"West Coast time or East Coast time?"

Apparently, some supporters were going to be on the Sunday morning shows saying Joe should stay in, and we didn't want them to be blindsided by questions from news anchors who'd heard the news at daybreak.

Meanwhile, Joe still had to do the job of governing. He had an important foreign policy call—we later learned it was with a Slavic diplomat, negotiating for the release of hostages being held in Russia. The rain had cleared, and it promised to be another beautiful day at the beach. I steeled myself for the hours ahead.

When Joe was off the phone, we reconvened.

Without a discussion, Joe said, "Okay, I'm ready to do this. Let's get this thing done." He had made his decision.

The plan was to start making notification calls and to release the letter sometime after noon.

I wanted the family to be told before anyone else. Hunter said he'd take care of notifying his girls. Joe wanted to call his sister and brother. I called Ashley. When I told her the news, she was heartbroken. "Why? Is Dad okay? Did something happen? He can win! Why is he getting out?"

I told her that Joe had to make his own decisions, and he wanted to do what was best for the party.

Joe's siblings called to tell him about all the people supporting him. He told them he was dropping out and read them the letter. Then he called Jen O'Malley Dillon, told her about his decision, and read it to her, too. It was a heartfelt conversation—she had been fighting so hard for Joe, for so long—then, she put the wheels in motion to tell the world.

When Joe reached Kamala, she was at home at the vice president's residence. Her campaign staff was in the pool house. With the call on speaker and the rest of us seated with him around the table, Joe told her that he'd made the decision to drop out of the race.

"Oh my God, Joe," she said. "Are you *sure*?"

Joe read the letter to her. He said he'd pass resources to her and support her as nominee. Her candidacy would be historic.

"Let me say, I love you to death," Kamala said. "Are you sure you feel right?"

"The leaders have made the decision for the party," he said. "It's about my age."

She switched immediately into what I could only imagine to be her courtroom prosecutor mode.

"So how are you thinking about timing?" she asked.

"The letter goes out today," he said. "I have to do it soon."

"Today? Okay, so the concern I have is what's the process of saying whether you support me? Any gap in time will have people speculating. We need to control this more."

Mike weighed in: "We need time. Early tomorrow morning, the president can send a letter to the Dems saying that you have his support."

They kept describing the way they were planning to go out with the news, and she kept pushing back hard, urging him to do it faster: "How soon can you endorse me, Joe?"

"By tomorrow, probably," he replied.

"No—you know these Democrats, and they will be up to mischief. I want it sooner."

"I'll call you back when I figure this out," Joe said.

"Could you do it soon? Say, in twenty minutes?"

I walked out of the room.

There were more calls that day, so many calls. I went in and out of the room, listening for a while and then taking time to myself before returning to see what was happening next.

Jim Clyburn, a loyal friend through the years, encouraged Joe to get out there and say he supported Kamala before the questions about his successor started. He wanted Joe to be proactive. "Take control of the process," Jim advised. Jim always gave Joe sage advice. Joe was close to him and his late wife, Emily, who held a special place in our hearts. It's hard to have true friends in Washington, but Jim was one of them. Still is.

"I have a letter that's going out," Joe said. "Then I'll make a statement that I support Kamala."

Listening on speakerphone, Mike clarified, "A separate tweet, 'I support Kamala Harris,' will go out after the letter."

In his bones, Joe believed that he could win and knew he could serve. To give that up and walk away from the public service role that was his life's purpose was a choice he made entirely in the interest of serving his party and assuaging his country. Pulling out of the race was yet another moment in Joe's life when everything changed in an instant. As he had so many times before, he rose to the challenge and handled it with grace. Watching him on the phone that day, somber and resolute, I thought, *I wish people could see this statesman.*

The letter went out at 1:46 p.m.

"It has been the greatest honor of my life to serve as your President," Joe said in the letter. "And while it has been my intention to seek reelection, I believe it is in the best interest of my party and the country for me to stand down and to focus solely on fulfilling my duties as President for the remainder of my term."

The house was filling up. Steve, Mike, Richard, Jacob, Anthony, and Annie were all there as Joe called his senior staff. Ashley drove down, too.

He told his senior staff that it had become hard to get the campaign on track after the debate. He said that he'd made the decision not to run. He read them the letter. He said once the letter went out that soon after he would send out a tweet to endorse Kamala.

On the call, Joe's chief of staff, Jeff Zients, told him, "You've been an extraordinary president. We have more to do."

"A lot of work left to do," Joe said. "I'll need your help."

Whenever anyone pushed back on his choice, he said, simply, "I shouldn't have to take on Democrats to be the nominee."

That was it. It was done.

Fifteen minutes later, Kamala called. She had been joined by her aides Sheila Nix and Lorraine Voles and their staff.

Joe said again that there would be coordination between his team and hers.

"Okay, that's great," she said. "I want to be in the strongest position. I believe in you. I want to be a part of your legacy."

Steve jumped in and mentioned that the tweets supporting her would be going out. "It will move quickly," he said.

"We are students of history," said Kamala. "We control how this narrative unfolds. It's significant how this transfer takes place."

Steve: "Yes, this preserves that."

She was not wrong to worry about the party's plans. Many Democrats wanted to explore various options for Joe's replacement. But Joe was always going to support his vice president. He did not even consider giving his delegates to anyone else.

As promised, Joe followed up his announcement about leaving the race with an endorsement of Kamala. At 2:13 p.m., about half an hour after leaving the race, he posted on X:

> My fellow Democrats, I have decided not to accept the nomination and to focus all my energies on my duties as President for the remainder of my term. My very first decision as the party nominee in 2020 was to pick Kamala Harris as my Vice President. And it's been the best decision I've made. Today I want to offer my full support and endorsement for Kamala to be the nominee of our party this year. Democrats—it's time to come together and beat Trump. Let's do this.

I didn't want my staff to hear it from anyone but me, so I called them. After sharing the news, I told them that we had to do whatever we could to help Kamala win.

That night, as we got ready for bed, I asked Joe, "How are you feeling about the decision?"

He appeared strong and resigned. He took my hand and said, "Jilly, I had no choice."

CHAPTER 32

For my remaining months as First Lady, I had three goals: to do whatever it took to get Kamala elected, to thank everyone who had supported us, and to close up my initiatives. All the while, I savored each moment left in the White House. It had truly been my honor to be its caretaker.

For much of that August, I found myself still having that unsteady feeling you get when you step onto a plank between solid ground and a dock.

I heard myself saying things like "Thursday? Today is *Thursday*?"

When I turned on the television just for a minute to catch the news about America's Olympic teams before going to cycle class, all of a sudden, there was breaking news: Evan Gershkovich was being released, and Paul Whelan, and several more.

Most of the time, I couldn't bear to turn on the news to see anything political because I was still feeling battered by the way in which the Democrats had spoken about Joe, but I was glad I'd caught that news segment. It was a reminder of Joe's effectiveness. Those calls he had been making on the morning of the day he ended his campaign, as well as all his years of hard work, had yielded real results. Families were being reunited because of his efforts. I felt a surge of hope for the world.

The Summer Olympics, too, were inspiring. I brought my grandkids along with me to the games in Paris, and one day I was able to steal a moment with them away from my official duties. As we ate lunch together, I looked around the table and thought about how proud I was of who they had become. Hunter was finishing boarding school and applying to U. Penn. He and his sister, Natalie, who was already there, looked forward to being at school together, an idea I loved. Maisy was traveling and finding she had so many creative talents, from visual art to working as a chef. They had all become resilient and independent, and I was so proud of each of them.

Throughout my time at the games, I was heartened by all the world leaders who had such positive and kind comments about Joe: Greece, Kosovo, Belgium, Romania, France, Ireland, Finland, Germany . . . They kept coming up to me and saying, "Thank you for your service."

Each time I heard it, I found myself moved by their tributes. I wished Joe could have been there to hear how warmly the heads of state spoke of him.

When I attended a reception on the Champs-Élysées, German Chancellor Olaf Scholz rushed up to ask me how Joe was, telling me how much he admired him and all the work they'd done together. His comments were warm and heartfelt. I clasped his hands and thanked him. I told him Joe felt the same way—that in fact he'd told me to find the chancellor that day to thank him for his loyalty and his integrity. Their feelings for each other were genuine, and the friendship meant so much to Joe—and to me, too.

When I wasn't seeing to my duties as First Lady that fall, I was out on the road for Kamala. She seized the opportunity and was giving it everything she had. It was exciting to see the crowds she was drawing and the hope that people felt.

"I'm going to be there for you," Joe had told her when he withdrew from the race.

"You're stuck with me like gum on a shoe," she'd joked back.

I found Doug to be great company. We went to SoulCycle together and cohosted countless events. I loved that he'd become a teacher. He'd taken a job at Georgetown, and we were able to discuss strategies. When he was grading papers, I suggested he put the positive comments first—something that, as a lawyer, he didn't necessarily think to do.

He was a real person, a gift that at times in Washington can feel like a life raft on the ocean. One time at an event, someone who we knew hated us came up and said, "It's so nice to see you!" Doug smiled big, said, "You, too!" Then, under his breath, so only I could hear, he said, "*Bullshit.*"

As I hit the trail with Doug and on my own, I campaigned hard.

On September 23, 2024, I went to the United Nations in New York to host a leaders' reception for the UN General Assembly. I also delivered remarks at the UN's LGBTI Core Group's "Leaving No One Behind: An Inclusive Future for All" event, spoke with USAID and UNICEF about protecting children from lead exposure, and appeared as part of the summit of First Ladies and Gentlemen gathering to discuss improvements in children's safety. I was able to briefly visit with Ukraine's Olena Zelenska, and noted how she'd blossomed from a reluctant figurehead into a strong advocate, taking every opportunity to fight for her people.

That evening at the UN, I was in conversation with Chelsea Clinton and Dr. Valerie Montgomery Rice before a large crowd as part of the Clinton Global Initiative. We spoke about the ways in which women's health had been routinely neglected.

As the talk ended, "Hail to the Chief" started playing. That was odd. This usually only happened to announce the arrival of the president.

Hillary Clinton walked out. After her, Bill Clinton appeared—escorting Joe! Everyone leapt to their feet for a spontaneous standing ovation. Onstage, Joe hugged me, and then Bill did, too.

"Ladies and gentlemen, we thought the two doctors deserved a surprise," Bill said. He talked about how much good work Joe had done and then presented him with an unexpected honor: the 2024 Clinton Global Citizen Award. In accepting, Joe said my work on women's health research would go down as one of the administration's significant programs.

The award meant so much to Joe, and I think the chance to do him a kindness at a difficult time meant a lot to Bill and Hillary. The whole week was bittersweet. The leaders and spouses thanked us over and over for the tone of congeniality and promise set by Joe's administration.

A couple of days later, the final UN General Assembly reception was held at the Metropolitan Museum of Art. Joe ran late, as usual, so we missed going into the crowd. It was probably a blessing, because how could Joe say hello to everyone the way he always wanted to? Later that night, we stood for almost two hours greeting leaders on the hard marble floor. I leaned over and joked to Joe, "Perhaps this all worked out for the best. Would you want to be standing on this hard floor at eighty-six? Maybe not."

I attended the inauguration of Claudia Sheinbaum in Mexico on October 1. A woman president—might that be a harbinger for the US?

The love and support for the outgoing president, Andrés Manuel Lopéz Obrador, was overwhelming. Half the Mexican chamber shouted, "We love the president!" before Obrador entered. Then they enveloped him as he walked to the front, chanting *"¡Es un honor estar con Obrador!"* ("It's an honor to be with Obrador!"), raising their fists.

Obrador's wife, Beatriz Gutiérrez Müller, came into the balcony where I was sitting to greet me. We embraced and she said, "This is going to be so hard, harder than you think."

She was speaking to me woman-to-woman, and I felt a swell of emotion. Below us, Claudia entered the hall to thunderous chanting. Obrador passed the sash to her, and she gave an impressive, impassioned speech on her plans for reform. She thanked me in her speech and noted, "Politics is made with love, not hate." Indeed. Never more evident. Thousands of people lined the streets, celebrating. Music was everywhere. It was so nice to see that kind of positivity and energy, a reminder that politics could actually be fun.

On November 4, I was in Durham, North Carolina, for my final day on the road in support of the Harris-Walz ticket. As usual, my staff was there to support me. Jordan Montoya made sure I had everything I needed: my speeches, my schedule, the right clothing for the events. Marty Browne, my trip director, kept us all on time, and upbeat with his dry sense of humor. I couldn't have done this without them.

I love Tim and Gwen Walz. We'd known them for years. Joe and I had done events with the couple in Minnesota during COVID, so they were familiar faces. They were such down-to-earth, good people, and Tim and Gwen and I had always bonded as fellow educators. Our time together was easy. We all had so many stories about being in the classroom. I always say that when you meet a teacher, you feel like you're talking to a member of your family—because you are.

One of my last lines that afternoon: "It's been my life's honor to be your First Lady."

"You're going to make me emotional!" I scolded the crowd when they applauded. "And I have to say this last line." I composed myself and said it: "Let's elect Kamala Harris and Tim Walz."

On November 5, 2024, I wore a favorite cranberry-colored pantsuit to vote at Tatnall, a private prep school by our house in Wilmington. My outfit was the color of the leaves outside my window. I did not anticipate that the reddish fabric would be taken as a sign by some MAGA folks that I had voted Republican. (I had not.)

After casting my ballot for Kamala, I went to visit Beau's grave at St. Joseph on the Brandywine Cemetery. Sitting on the grass, looking at his headstone with its twin crosses and the words "Father, Husband, Brother, Son," I noticed a tree bent toward his grave, just as in life people were drawn to Beau and his goodness. At the cemetery that day, for the first time in a very long time, I let myself cry. For Beau, our beautiful son who had died far too young. For Joe, who'd made a hard choice. For all the tragedies I'd borne witness to in the prior years. I tidied the flowers, flags, and stones, and allowed myself a moment of reflection, possibly the first deep breath in and out I'd experienced in months.

CHAPTER 33

Going into election night, I believed that Kamala was going to win. For the White House senior staff that evening, I arranged for an early White House gathering. We invited everyone upstairs for drinks in the Yellow Oval, usually used for foreign dignitaries, and then out onto the Truman Balcony to take in the view. A traditional Biden dinner was served downstairs in the Blue Room—chicken parm and pasta, the same thing we always served on meaningful family nights. It was the same meal we'd shared at our Chain Bridge house in 2019 for our first campaign staff meal.

The plan was that we'd eat early so that afterward, everyone could head over to celebrate with Vice President Harris and her team at Howard University. We expected that the results would be coming in late into the night, that ballots might not be counted for days.

TVs were on in the background but on low, and very early—too early—it appeared to be going a certain way.

Indiana came in red at 9:05. A minute later: Kentucky. Twenty-five minutes later: West Virginia. At around ten p.m., the former president took Alabama, Mississippi, Oklahoma, Tennessee, Florida, South Carolina, Arkansas . . . Harris only had Vermont, New Jersey,

Connecticut, Maryland, Massachusetts, and Rhode Island. Electoral votes: 101 to 49.

A flood of calls were coming into the White House. People were concerned.

"This is not good," they were saying. "We don't have the numbers."

At dawn, I woke to Willow pawing at me to get up. I had planned to sleep a little later and to go to an exercise class at nine, but she demanded breakfast. A few hours earlier, I'd heard Joe climbing into bed. I noticed that he didn't wake me to say Kamala had won, and as I drifted back to sleep, I decided that the decision wasn't in yet. After all, we'd had to wait almost five days before Joe was declared the winner in 2020.

As I put food in front of Willow, petted her, and said, "You're welcome," I heard my phone ping.

"You up?" Anthony texted.

"Yes . . . why?" I responded. In that moment, I knew. Waiting for my first cup of coffee to finish brewing, I scrolled through dozens and dozens of text messages that had come through from friends and family while I'd been sleeping:

"I feel sick."

"I can't believe it."

"Oh, Jill."

I grabbed my coffee and walked into the bedroom to find that Joe was awake. I sat down next to him on the bed.

"Joe, do you know he won?" I asked.

"Yes," he said.

In a daze, I began returning calls from the grandkids, who were beside themselves.

Everyone on TV was offering explanations for Kamala's loss. Prices were high. She was accused of seeming inauthentic. A lot of people weren't ready for a woman president. An anti-trans ad had bombarded swing states. Pick your depressing reason.

The first time I saw Kamala after the election was on Veterans Day in the Diplomatic Reception Room at the White House. Joe and I met her there to drive out to Arlington National Cemetery together—a reminder of our shared commitment to putting service before self. Side by side, she and Joe laid a wreath at the Tomb of the Unknown Soldier.

I vowed to wrap things up as well as I could, and to do as much as I could with the rest of my time. I hosted a summit on women's health. I traveled to the Middle East. I kept teaching full-time, and I kept up with my duties as First Lady. I tried to uphold the traditions around the transition. I invited Melania for tea. She declined, citing a prior commitment.

For our last holiday in the White House, 2024, we had to plan the holiday decor without knowing what would happen with the election. I wanted to keep it simple because of the widespread fear that if the election was called for the Democrats, the result might be a civil war. Yes, we really did have that concern. And, at the time, world peace felt very far away. So, for our theme that year, I chose "A Season of Peace and Light." We filled the whole main hallway with a thousand white paper doves, as if filling the White House with warmth and beauty and symbols of reconciliation could create a sense of harmony that would carry into the new administration.

Exhausted at the end of a holiday party, I was walking down the festive hall toward the elevator when Kamala came up to me.

"I love you, Jill Biden," she said.

I felt tenderly toward her as we watched everything wind down around us.

"I love you, too," I said.

I'd felt in my bones that the next residents of this house would be Kamala and Doug.

Those final few weeks were a whirlwind of packing and taking care of a long list of agenda items surrounding the transition. If I'd thought winning would satisfy Joe's opponent, that it would cause him to forget about us, I'd have been mistaken. Nearly every day I heard a new conspiracy theory involving our family. One was that in Joe's final year in office, I was leading cabinet meetings. On September, 20, 2024, I dropped by one cabinet meeting to give opening remarks on women's health research for five minutes. As soon as I'd given my remarks, I left. Another theory had it that I pushed Joe to run and kept him in the race to stay in my role. This, too, is incorrect.

The question of pardons had weighed heavily on Joe, and I'd watched him struggle with it for months. Joe's senior advisors told him not to pardon Hunter, and Joe had not planned to. Then he caught wind of just how vindictive the incoming administration was likely to be. Joe also came to believe that it was unfair how Hunter had been taken to trial for something that under other circumstances would have been a minor infraction resulting in a quick plea deal. We'd seen Hunter, now several years sober, pay the price for his former notoriety, becoming practically unemployable. Right-wing news hosts used him as a reliable ratings-boosting punching bag, and the paparazzi stalked his every move.

After the guilty verdict, when it became clear that Hunter might be facing prison time, and when others in Joe's orbit appeared to be vulnerable to unjust, politically motivated punishments, Joe made the call. Advisors protested, but Joe remained adamant that he would not let his family be punished for his political life.

Once Joe and I had packed up, the White House looked barren. My plants were gone. The paintings I'd chosen for the walls had been removed. It actually made it easier to leave, seeing how impersonal the house had become. I hardly saw Joe during that time because he and his aides were trying to finish up so many things and to shore up as much of his legacy as they could.

The incoming president would hang a picture of an autopen machine to represent President Joe Biden. Joe's political rivals would later insist Joe hadn't known what was happening at the end of his administration, or that his aides were running the White House—or I was. All of this seemed too absurd to even dignify with a denial. I had never even seen an autopen. Before it existed, a secretary would copy the president's signature. It wasn't nefarious; there was just too much paper for any one person. Joe worked long hours in those weeks making one decision after the other, just as he had before the election.

One bright spot in Joe's schedule on his way out was the bestowal of the Medal of Freedom to a group of people who'd made America better. That event always has a bit of magic to it, and that year it felt particularly warm and heartfelt, with tributes to José Andrés, Bono, Hillary Clinton, Magic Johnson, Ralph Lauren, and Anna Wintour. I was so proud that our administration was honoring great people who had accomplished the extraordinary. Even more, I loved watching the faces of their family members—so proud of their loved one. I, too, had experienced the joy of watching as Joe received the Medal of Freedom with Distinction from Barack in 2017. It's definitely an emotional, reflective moment—you can't help but feel a lump in your throat.

There were quieter joys, too. When our grandson Beau, who lived in Southern California, came to DC for the holidays, he found the snow new and exciting. I took him out to the Rose Garden to make a snowman. The chef, Tommy, brought out vegetables from the refrigerator—a carrot for a nose, beets for the eyes. Someone produced a scarf, and just like that: the perfect snowman. Little Beau was mesmerized. I also showed him the White House Children's Garden, where his handprints and the bronze handprints of presidents' grandchildren since the 1960s have been encased in stones on the patio. I always enjoyed it as a way to remember the special relationship between families who have lived at the White House, whether Republican or Democrat.

That connection became clearer to me toward the end of our term as various former inhabitants came to visit what had been their childhood home. Chelsea Clinton brought her children to see it. One was a little prodigy and rattled off presidential history—no surprise to me, having seen how bright Chelsea was at that age.

That final month, we helped host the state funeral of Jimmy Carter, including a dinner at the White House for fifty-five members of the Carter family. At the funeral, Joe gave a beautiful eulogy, during which he told the story of a visit he and I made to see the Carters in Plains, Georgia, in April 2021. They'd been living there in that redbrick house together for seventy-seven years. When we saw them, they were cheerful, if frail. At Rosalynn's funeral in November 2023, it was clear that Jimmy didn't have much time left. However, his mind was still connected to the world around him. In a private moment, he whispered "I love you" to us, the last thing we'd hear him say.

On our last night at the White House, January 19, 2025, we said goodbye to the staff, which was heartbreaking. We had just returned that day from South Carolina—the same place where Joe's presidential campaign had truly begun. Now we were bidding farewell to so many good friends and people we loved. When I headed up to our room, Joe was still with his staff finishing off his list of pardons and being briefed on the next day's activity. I lit the fire and tried to enjoy one last evening in that beautiful room, but I couldn't stay awake. I fell asleep full of gratitude, but also anxious for what the next day would bring, as the president-elect prepared to return like some kind of avenging spirit.

CHAPTER 34

God, Inauguration Day was cold. During the week leading up to it, I watched the huge flakes of snow cascade past the windows of the White House, a view I was trying to enjoy as much as possible before leaving it. In those final days, I got up early in the morning when the residence was uncharacteristically void of people—waiters, valets, Secret Service, staff, and family. I used the time alone to absorb my feelings of appreciation and loss. I'd take pictures on my phone of the architectural details that I didn't want to forget. Plus, it gave me time to reflect.

One natural phenomenon that can be witnessed near the White House on any given day is a murmuration of starlings swirling together. I would watch in amazement from the Truman Balcony as thousands and thousands of birds ebbed and flowed through the sky, as if dancing to a silent symphony only they could hear. There were so many beautiful aspects to the White House. I tried to pay attention and never to take any of it for granted.

That final morning in the White House, I woke up, looked at the frosted windows in the residence, and thought, *Hmm, the perfect place for a message*. The heating vents underneath the palladium windows formed crystals in the windowpanes and created a crystalline cocoon. Where we sat to watch TV was entirely covered by a thin, watery cover—like the one you see from steam on a shower door. I could write something, and it was unlikely anyone would notice until the next morning.

Tempting. The residence staff wouldn't observe it because the sun would have warmed the glass by the time they would come into that part of the house. Yes! I would write it with my finger in the steam. I looked at the message for a few moments . . . *Should I let it remain?* Finally, I left that room for the last time, heading upstairs to get ready.

Ralph Lauren and his team had made available two suits to choose from—one blue, one purple. The blue was an obvious political choice, but purple signified unity. I still believed in that. I loved that two-piece outfit with its purple coat and gloves and matching purse. I felt good in it—confident. The son of Belarusian immigrants, Ralph had started his business by selling ties. He often dressed Republicans as well as Democrats because his is an iconic American brand—not red or blue, but a tribute to the pride that Americans feel in their country.

On Inauguration Day, following tradition down to the minute, the inauguration committee was gathering in the Blue Room for coffee and tea, waiting for the president-elect to arrive.

First Kamala and Doug greeted Vice President–Elect J. D. Vance and his wife, Usha, and brought them inside. When Donald and Melania's car pulled up and they got out, Joe and I went to greet them. There were pleasantries.

The new president asked where we were going to live, and I said, "Delaware, Philadelphia, or LA."

"That's an interesting choice," he said.

We smiled, posed for the obligatory picture, and then headed inside for tea.

As is customary, the First Ladies were to ride to the inauguration together, and we were assigned to a car with a member of the committee. I don't know how long this has been tradition, but it certainly does make it easier in cases of awkwardness.

John Bessler, Amy Klobuchar's husband, must have drawn the shortest of all possible straws, because he got what was arguably one of the trickiest assignments: escorting Melania and me to the inauguration. The presidents' car was likely frosty, too, but at least they'd spent considerable time in each other's company. This would be one of few interactions Melania and I had ever had. Melania hadn't invited me for tea in 2021; she'd turned down my invitation in 2024. We met briefly at both Carter funerals. Each year, I sent her a birthday card, as I sent one to every other living First Lady.

As I understood it, Melania blamed Joe personally for the FBI searching through her private spaces at Mar-a-Lago. I had compassion for her, having been subject to the same kind of search. I knew how distressing it was to have agents rummage through your underwear drawer.

Poor John had to figure out how to break the tension and find some path to relative peace in the course of that drive. He'd always struck me as a quiet, reserved Midwestern guy, but as soon as we got in, he began chatting away, pelting us both with questions. My impression was that Amy, who I'd always liked very much, had told him to put some pep in his step when he rode with us.

"Where's Barron in school?" John asked.

"NYU," Melania said, looking out the window, clearly about to point to the clouds as a way of segueing to a neutral topic.

"Where does he live?" John said.

"He has a floor in Trump Tower," she said.

"Is he having fun?" said John.

"He goes to school, attends class, and they bring him back. He doesn't see many friends at school."

"Does he have lots of friends?" John said.

Melania kept trying to switch the topic to the weather.

"Yes, he has friends from high school," she said, noting how cold and windy it had been.

John moved on to talking about an Impressionists show at the National Gallery that had just closed. He said that people had been flying in from all over to see it. I looked it up on my phone and said that it did seem like a great show; I was sorry to have missed it.

I asked Melania about her father, because her mother had recently died.

She said he was doing okay, and he was there with them, then said, "But you know, it's only been a year."

I tried to get with Melania's weather-only program. I said I felt bad for the military dogs we passed along the route because of the cold.

"Do you have a dog?" John asked Melania.

"No, no, we never had a dog," she said. "I asked Barron several times, but he said no, he didn't want a dog."

"Well, where did you grow up in Slovenia?" he asked. They discussed an area of the country where John had been.

We arrived at the Capitol. We made a quick stop at Republican Senator Chuck Grassley's office before walking into the rotunda. First the Clintons walked in, then the Bushes, then Barack. When the inaugural speech grew particularly bombastic, I nudged Doug Emhoff to make sure that he'd heard it, too. At the new president's mention of renaming the Gulf of Mexico the "Gulf of America," Hillary Clinton burst out laughing.

After it was over and official, the new president said to me, "If Joe ever needs anything, call me!"

Before leaving the White House that morning, I'd handwritten Melania a note wishing her well. I put it on the desk, per tradition, and I had a vase of flowers brought up to leave with the note. I later learned that a member of the White House staff slipped a letter underneath mine. (The residence staff typically stays on from one administration to another.) At least the note didn't go on top, I guess, but the presumption of the gesture—trying to catch the attention of the incoming First Lady by insinuating oneself into a private historic tradition between two women—still frosted me.

Then, after the inauguration, we were climbing into what we'd come to know as Marine One. Joe and I held hands as we took off. We'd taken that flight many times; this was the last one. I looked out over DC.

The helicopter circled once over the White House and then out to Joint Base Andrews. When we passed the Capitol, I felt Joe's body language shift. That was his home for thirty-six years; how huge it must have felt to be leaving.

"Wow, Joe, this is really full circle," I said. He squeezed my hand.

When we arrived at Andrews, music was playing. Hundreds of people were there waiting in the cold in the airplane hangar, including former staff and their families. Joe climbed onstage and gave a final goodbye.

Then we boarded the presidential plane for the last time, headed to Santa Ynez, California, to stay at the ranch of our friends Joe and

Sarah Kiani for a few days. On board, the crew served us a special meal they knew we'd love, a hometown favorite: Philly cheesesteaks. When wc landed, the staff was emotional.

It was a balm to see our friends. The Kianis made us feel so welcome. When we walked into their guest house, we saw they'd set out a big cheese tray and soda for Joe and wine for me. There were flowers in every room. What a relief to have nothing to do for that week but walk through beautiful vineyards and have big meals with our family.

And yet those first days of what I began to call the afterlife were difficult. When we went into town, we saw big MAGA pickup parades. We had to turn the TV off because when it was on, we saw that the new administration was undoing everything we'd fought for. I found walking in nature healing. Joe didn't; he was on the phone tracking everything, trying to figure out if there was any way he could help.

After a week, we went back to Delaware to start our life after the White House.

CHAPTER 35

On October 20, 2025, the last day of Joe's radiation therapy, he rang the hospital bell and was presented with a coconut cake, his favorite.

Everywhere I go—the gym, the grocery store, the beach—I am stopped by people telling me horror stories.

"I'm losing my FEMA job—my whole life has been devoted to saving people!"

"My cancer research lab is closing—all that training, all that work, for what?"

"I can't afford groceries to feed my family. Eggs are eight dollars!"

"My partner—an upstanding, tax-paying member of our community who's lived here forty years—is being deported. What do I tell our children?"

What can I say? I hug them. I quote Dr. Martin Luther King Jr. on the arc of history bending toward justice. These are the things I tell myself, too, when I wake up in the middle of the night ruminating on everything I've heard, and wondering how the changes will continue to affect my family and all Americans.

The new president has been making good on many of his most extreme campaign promises—rounding up immigrants and sending them to deportation camps in foreign countries, pulling the plug on humanitarian aid around the world, firing swaths of government workers and scientists like the ones I've met in the course of my advocacy for women's health. How to even keep track of all the changes, much less make any sense of them? So many people who'd devoted their whole lives to trying to make us safer and healthier are being cast aside.

During the demolition of the East Wing—which had architectural elements put in place by President Thomas Jefferson in 1805, President Theodore Roosevelt in 1902, and FDR in 1942, not to mention Lady Bird Johnson's exquisite garden dedicated in 1965 to Jacqueline Kennedy—I received pictures of the destruction step by step from people in DC. I could barely look. The social offices, gutted. The military office, flattened. What had been my office, gone. A major landmark and historic treasure was being treated like an extreme fixer-upper on HGTV's *Property Brothers*. It wasn't the loss of the blue-and-white-striped drapes, the velvet sofa, the bookshelves filled with memorabilia that pained me—it was the symbolic bulldozing of history and the eradication of institutional memory.

I kept thinking of everyone across the country who took pride in that building. I felt a sense of loss and grief with every blow from the wrecking ball. The innards of the East Wing were spread out for everyone to see, like a rare and precious animal that had been hunted down and killed.

Whenever life became difficult, I longed to sit by the ocean. For decades, when we went to Rehoboth Beach for a week or so in the summer, we rented a house or stayed with friends. I'd dreamed of a place of our own by the water that the grandkids would love to visit. Joe always promised me that one day we'd be able to buy our own place, and in 2017, he made good. He hung a sign on the front of the house that reads A PROMISE KEPT.

I loved everything about this house from the moment I first saw it—the kitchen, the fireplaces, even the furniture. The property lot backed a protected park, so we knew that we'd never lose our view. The neighbors were friendly but not *too* friendly—perfect.

"This is it!" I said on the first day of house hunting.

"What do you mean?" Joe said. "We haven't even seen any other houses."

"Well, it doesn't matter," I said. "I love *this* house."

Before committing to it, Joe made me go see *twenty-five other houses*. He'd designed our Wilmington home, and he found looking at houses to be a fun opportunity to engage with his love of architecture. *Finally*, after Joe had looked at *every house on the market*, he conceded that the first place was the one for us, and we negotiated to buy the house with all its contents. The couple who'd owned it basically just gave us the keys, and we moved in. Since then, I've replaced a rug here and there as they've worn out, but it's more or less the same house I saw on that tour, now almost a decade ago.

I particularly love the first light coming through the windows in our top-floor bedroom. I love to see the sunrise, and sometimes I set the clock so that I don't miss it. Joe will pull down his eye mask and mutter, "Too bright."

I reply, "But, Joe, it's so beautiful!" I can see the ocean right from our room. If it's very quiet, I can even hear the waves.

That final flight away from Washington feels like ages ago even though it's been almost no time at all. Willow wakes me up at six each morning purring, and throwing her now slightly plump gray body against me. She's definitely enjoying the change of scenery. She's filled out here at the beach house, and spends her days prowling around the yard or lying in sunbeams.

Life has slowed down. For years, our friends would come to Washington on Independence Day for epic festivities of marching bands, fireworks, barbecuing, and kids everywhere waving sparklers. Joe and I spent last Fourth of July weekend at Naomi's in California. Because of the fires, the city used drones rather than fireworks. In her backyard around the pool, we watched the colorful lights flash silently off in the distant sky.

I've been trying to see this time as just one more life stage, like having a new baby or becoming an empty nester. I had been so structured for most of my life, and now there's no consistent household schedule. Joe likes to stay up late. I'm often in bed by 9:30, ten o'clock. He sleeps in; I'm off to an exercise class by nine. I even lay out my clothes the night before—it's the teacher in me.

Growing old together as a couple is full of both joys and challenges. Getting older has caused me to ask big questions about our shared life: *Who are you now? Who am I? Who are we? Look at these things that we created together. What might be left for us to build?*

Opposites really do attract. I love to be by myself and prefer quiet. Joe loves a crowd, and at home, he has the TV on or he's on the phone. When he was in office, Joe's press team was always trying to rein him in because he would talk to anyone for hours. He handed out his cell number to people on rope lines and would take calls after dinner to talk about grief or the issues of the day. Joe would talk to random reporters who happened to catch him on the phone, regardless of the call schedule the team had set up. It got to the point where he agreed to let them gatekeep because without them, I swear he'd pick up any call that came in, at any hour.

Joe even picks up *my* phone. If I'm in the other room doing something and my phone rings, he'll pick it up and chat away until he says, ten minutes later, "Your sister's on the phone for you!"

If he's in the shower and his phone rings, I always call out to him, "Your phone's ringing!"

He will say, "Well, why don't you answer it?"

I'll say, "Because I'm not you!"

Beau's death is always with us. Ever since, Mother's Day has been hard for me. How can you be happy to celebrate motherhood when one of your children is gone? That day still always makes me feel bone-sad. Yes, in his loss, we found purpose. Yes, we support cancer efforts in honor of his memory, and we cherish Natalie and Hunter, who remind us so powerfully of him. But some nights before we close our eyes, I still say, "Joe, I miss Beau," and he says, "Yes, I do, too."

Joe and the boys were always so simpatico, I don't think it ever occurred to Joe to develop many other friendships outside the family. That's another reason why Beau's death was so monumental for him and Hunter. His absence is felt in the loss of one of Joe's closest friendships as well as the unfathomable loss of a child. Because of Joe's age, a lot of his friends are gone. I keep saying to him, "Call so-and-so! Do this, do that!" But to him, it doesn't feel natural calling someone and saying, "Hey, are you free tomorrow for lunch?"

One thing I've learned from having sisters is that friendships and relationships are important, and you have to work at them. All through my marriage, all through my life, I've always made sure to have good girlfriends. There's your book friend who you love, and there's your gardening friend who you love. These old friends have been getting me through this uncertain time of life, even if sometimes I look around and say, "Wait, where did all these white-haired people come from?"

One of my good friends recently said she'd joined a mah jong club. I recoiled. "Mah jong?" I said. "That's for old people!"

I'm seventy-four.

Clearly, I've found it challenging to consider slowing down, much less to ponder my own mortality.

Years before Queen Elizabeth died, Joe and I were approached by the national security team in reference to something called Operation London Bridge. The operation was preplanning the queen's funeral. They wanted us to approve a long statement that would be released upon the queen's death, ending with, "We send our deepest condolences to the Royal Family, who are not only mourning their Queen, but their dear mother, grandmother, and great-grandmother. Her legacy will loom large in the pages of British history, and in the story of our world." It felt surreal to be mourning the living, and yet I recently learned that advance planning for Joe's funeral and mine is underway, too.

Before Joe's cancer diagnosis, I felt that, in spite of his being almost ten years older than me, I was the one running to catch up with him. He has always been my hero, my rock. The ways in which his illness has caused him to scale back have been a challenging adjustment for both of us.

Still, our work is not done. Joe has been jetting around giving talks and accepting honors. I've been exploring a position that would let me teach GED classes at a women's prison. What a fulfilling job that would be, to help women find a new path, one they can follow once they get out. I believe seeing them turn their lives around would give me hope, too.

Joe has always gone to Catholic Mass, but as a Presbyterian, I hesitated to attend with him because non-Catholics can't take Communion. I believe in my heart that Jesus wouldn't deny me the host, so I prefer to go to services where I'm able to receive it. Prayers, especially, are a part of how I connect to the people I love and the world around me. But with Beau's death, my faith was shaken. For more than a year, I watched my brave, strong, funny, bright young son fight brain cancer.

Chemotherapy, operation after operation, weight loss . . .

Still, I never gave up hope. As a mother, you can't. Despite what the doctors said, I believed he would live. In those final days, I made one last desperate prayer.

It went unanswered.

After Beau died, I felt betrayed by my faith. Broken.

My pastor wrote me emails, checking in and inviting me back to church . . . I just couldn't go. I couldn't even pray. I wondered if I would ever feel joy again.

I credit a moment in South Carolina in 2019 with helping me back to religion. At a Brookland Baptist Church service in West Columbia, at the start of Joe's presidential campaign, the pastor's wife, Robin Jackson, sat next to me and said, "I want to be your prayer partner."

". . . Okay?" I said.

I did not know what that meant. I hadn't heard the term before. But somehow, the way Robin spoke, it was if God were saying to me, "Jill, you've had enough time away. It's time to come home."

Robin and I arranged a call, and she gave me her number. We began talking once or twice a week, or checking in by text. That's been going on for six years now. She came to the White House several times with her daughter and grandchildren. I flew down for her birthday. What a gift she has been.

Poetry continues to comfort me, as it always has. The wise poet Nikki Giovanni wrote, "We love because it's the only true adventure." Falling in love with Joe is what gave me my three children, and gave me this huge, historic life I could never have imagined as a little girl biking around Willow Grove with my sisters.

Even as I feel dismayed by so much of what is happening, I refuse to give up faith in our shared future. To remind myself of how necessary it is to keep going, I find myself repeating Corinthians: "Love never gives up, never loses faith, is always hopeful, and endures through every circumstance."

I look at the circumstances I'm in today. Joe and I are here at our house at the beach, delighting in the rotating cast of visitors—children, grandchildren, sisters, friends. I drag everyone who will go along with me to my morning exercise classes.

There is so much good in the world, and I see it every day, whether I'm biking down to the beach with Little Beau, or sitting out on the deck in the mornings with Willow watching the sunrise. Most of all, I see goodness shining from the eyes of people I meet—that great majority of people who greet the world, messy as it is, with love and light. For all the hatred we see in the news, there are angels among us. I think of students who march across the stage for their diploma, earned against all odds; my fellow teachers who stay late grading papers and find ways to tend the lost lambs in their flock; the parents keeping faith in their children struggling through addiction; the military spouses packing up the household yet again because that's what their country needs them to do; the people entering lives of public service in order to build a better future.

Whenever I hear about how terrible the world is, I think of the nurses I've met in the course of Joe's cancer treatment. Every single time we arrived for Joe's radiation, day after day for five and a half weeks, we were greeted by the same beatific woman, Carly, standing at the end of the hallway, welcoming us with a huge smile on her face, reassuring us that everything would be okay. Because our country is full of people like her, I have faith that it will.

EPILOGUE

Five days into 2026, I'm ending this book the way I started it, with the death of a child: Tatiana Schlossberg, the daughter of Caroline Kennedy and Ed Schlossberg. At Thanksgiving, we all read her essay in *The New Yorker*. It was heartbreaking and tragic, knowing how hard she was fighting to live, having been diagnosed with a rare and aggressive form of acute myeloid leukemia right after giving birth to a daughter, Josie. I couldn't read the article straight through; I read it a little bit at a time.

Joe and I were honored to attend Tatiana's funeral. I knew the sorrow Caroline would feel every day for the rest of her life and wondered if in the course of the cancer treatment Caroline believed that a miracle would happen and her daughter would live. You never give up that hope. As a mother, you can't.

Caroline seemed so strong as she held her granddaugther, Josie, in her arms during the service. She possesses a quiet strength just like her mother, Jackie. Many people from our political universe attended. As the priest encouraged those in attendance to share the sign of peace, Joe walked two pews behind us and held out his hand to Nancy Pelosi. I instinctively knew what was happening without even turning around.

Peace.

Let's be friends.

They hugged and she kissed him on the cheek.

Old-school. Both of them. Putting the past behind them. One of Joe's greatest assets is his ability to forgive. I admire that about him.

The priest gave the final blessing. Jon Batiste stepped onto the altar with his harmonica to play "When the Saints Go Marching In."

Silence.

Sadness blanketed the congregation.

We moved slowly out of the church, returning to our lives. I'm hoping this year will be better than the last. While Joe might have some health challenges ahead, the doctors say that he is strong, that he will live out his natural life. As Dylan Thomas wrote, we will not go gentle into that good night, but rage, rage against the dying of the light.

So together we continue to rage against the dying light—fighting for democracy, battling cancer, working on women's health, building a presidential center, and spending time with our grandchildren. For as long as we can do this work, we will, and we will do it with the deepest gratitude for our family, for this country, for the opportunities we have been given, and for each other's love. We are blessed.

ACKNOWLEDGMENTS

I've always loved to read and write. Even as a young girl, books were a big part of my childhood. So I guess it's no surprise that I became an English teacher for forty years. For me, writing is a way to remember how I felt during certain times and to make sense of important events. Writing my way through my four years in the White House has given me new clarity and perspective, and I am grateful for the opportunity to do it.

I will always appreciate Deneen Howell and Emily Alden from Williams & Connolly for their insights and counsel in selecting and structuring the team for this project. Bob Barnett was right: Deneen is the best. Gallery Books publisher Jen Bergstrom, thank you for your constant encouragement and for making this project possible. To my beloved editor Aimée Bell, who also published Hunter's book, you promised to always have my back, and you have stayed true to your word. The Gallery team has taken such good care of me. Thank you to Sally Marvin, Jill Siegel, Emma Skeels, Abby Knudsen, Caroline Pallotta, Jamie Selzer, Julia Kott, and Felice Javit; you all made this book better.

Writing a memoir asks you to revisit moments that shaped you—

the joyful ones, the uncertain ones, the ones that still ache a little when remembered. Ada Calhoun listened not just to my words but to the pauses between them. That kind of listening is a gift. Ada understood that this story was never only about public life. It was about a family. About teaching. About love. About resilience. Ada honored the people in my life, whether it was those I met on the campaign trail or those I met in my classroom. Thank you, Ada, for your rigor as a writer and your tenderness as a collaborator. You asked the hard questions gently and protected the emotional truth of the story. I am deeply grateful for your partnership, your integrity, and your steady hand throughout this journey.

How do I begin to thank all the people who supported me during our time at the White House? I was always aware of how much planning and coordination went into everything I did each day. But as I sit down to write these thank-yous, I am in awe of the countless individuals who came together, contributing their talents to make our team truly remarkable.

To the White House residence staff who were able to transform a historic building into a home. Led by the example of Blair Downing, the chief usher, every interaction was met with warmth and grace. They became extended family to us, and we are forever grateful for the care they showed our family each and every day.

To the United States Secret Service: They went above and beyond to protect and care for my family—often at great sacrifice to their own families, missing holidays and life's everyday moments. Their dedication and service are beyond measure. May God bless them.

To the men and women of the White House Military Office and its supporting agencies—WHCA, WHMU, and WHTA—and to the flight crews across the Air Force and National Guard who carried us safely around the world: I thank them for their professionalism, their sacrifice, and their steadfast commitment. I have such deep admiration for their military service, and I treasured the time spent getting to know so many of them.

To the advance teams who worked tirelessly behind the scenes to ensure every detail of every visit was thoughtfully and meticulously planned: You don't always get the credit you deserve, but your work is indispensable to the mission.

My staff—from the campaigns to the White House—gave so much of themselves to this work, and I was fortunate to be surrounded by a team of fun, brilliant, and kind professionals. They are family. Thank you to Team Jill: Kristin Adams, Mala Adiga, Areeb Akbari, Elizabeth Alexander, Lexi Barrett, Nidhi Bouri, Marty Browne, Jasmine Byers, Patricia Camerota, Sheila Casey, Bonnie Casillas, Nelvis Castro, Lauren Chang, Stacy Choi, Vanessa Cobarrubias, John Cohill, Katherine DelGiudice, Daniela Diaz, Donovan Dixon, Nicholas Dockery, Megan Doherty, Kelsey Donohue, Rykia Dorsey, Zach Duffy, Manny Duran, Carlos Elizondo, Carly Faulkner, Iris Feldman, Asjia Garner, Brad Glazier, Charlie Goldensohn, Jon Groat, Camilo Haller, Liz Hart, Caitlin Healy, Jack Healy, Lydia Hecmanczuk, Yuwynn Ho, CJ Hoekenga, Nicole Jackson, Libby Jamison, Zaina Javaid, Candace Johnson, Venus Johnson, Max Katz, Catherine Kiani, Faith Kwentua, Michael LaRosa, Gina Lee, Janice Lee, Eduardo Levi, David Lienemann, Vanessa Lion, Patricia Liu, Kristin Lynch, Amber Macdonald, Rory Martin, Carolyn Mazure, Gionelly Mills, Jen Mishory, Jordan Montoya, Brie Moore, Emily Morgan, John Moylan, Himaja Nagireddy, Vinh Nguyen, David Nurnberg, Ally O'Connell, Keigo O'Haru, Julissa Reynoso Pantaleón, Sherice Perry, Jeannie Rangel, Colby Redmond, Shannon Ricchetti, Emma Riley, Mary Robbins, Drew Rodriguez, Kasey Rollins, John Scanlon, Melissa Schwartz, Peyton Schwartz, Erin Scott,

DJ Sigworth, Wayne Skinner, Cameron Smith, Meredith Smith, Tony Starks, Giancarlo Stefanoni, Emma Stopek, Nixie Strazza, Maureen Szemborski, Christine Thompson, Vanessa Valdivia, Garima Verma, Eryn Wagnon, Ellie Warner, Bridget Williams, Josh Woehr, Amber Wynne, and Ethan Yake.

I am grateful to Joe's West Wing staff and senior advisors for being such great partners. Your insight, commitment, and unwavering support helped create a positive impact that will last well beyond Joe's administration.

A special thank you to Anthony Bernal, who has been by my side for eighteen years. In this project, as in all things, I know he always has my best interests at heart. I trust him implicitly. Anthony, I'm thankful that I have you in my life.

I am a proud card-carrying union member. Becky Pringle, Randi Weingarten, and the members of the NEA and AFT are my family. Teaching isn't just our profession; it is our calling. Each of you answered that call. You believe that a better world is possible—and you make that world real, one student at a time.

After I left Delaware Technical Community College, President Mark Brainard built a student success center in my honor. I feel so proud to still remain part of that institution. At Northern Virginia Community College, Dean Jimmie McClellan was one of my greatest supporters and champions. He assembled a language arts department of men and women who were supportive of me as a colleague and beyond. Their kindness was immeasurable.

Many professors and staff helped me build a center to mentor women through to graduation. Thank you to our founders Azza Ahmed, Jean Braden, Linda Campos, Emily Chiles, Brenda Conerly, Martha Davis, Connie Ellsberg, Janet Giannotti, Pat Gordon, Beth

Harrison, Marjorie Kinnaman, Carolyn Lorente, Pat Lunt, Rachel Martin, Ginger Primus, Noemi Rosado-Roman, Judy Snyder, and Kathy Wax, as well as all the other women who were part of that group. We could not have accomplished all we did without the help of George Gabriel. We did good things together for our students.

To the women I've met, whether in my classroom or in my travels—I have loved connecting with all of you. Your tenacity and grit have inspired me to fight for you, every day—as Second and First Lady and beyond.

I'm hoping to continue my work in cancer and education and women's health. I am pleased to continue my advocacy as chair of the Women's Health Network at the Milken Institute. Esther Krofah, executive vice president of health at Milken, has continued to be my partner and mentor in this space. My admiration for her is endless—she's become a true friend. John Scanlon—who with Carolyn Mazure, Jennifer Klein, Katie Keith, Lina Volin, Suhasini Ravi, Dr. Tamara Allard, and Dr. Jennifer Robinson developed the White House Initiative on Women's Health Research—has helped me build my portfolio and knowledge. He's impressive and thorough in all he does.

Finally, I am fortunate to have so many friends and family who have been there for me always and who encouraged me to write this book.

To my children Hunter and Ashley, I am deeply grateful to you for giving me your support and advice as each chapter unfolded. You encouraged me to write my truth, my story. Your love—and Beau's—for me as your mother has been what I treasure above all else in my life. "I love you more." Always.

To each of my grandchildren, who have given me one of the most beautiful and fun parts of my life.

To my sisters—Jan, Bonny, Kim, and Kelly—who have always carried me.

Thanks to my friends, especially Mary Ann, Mary, Alicia, and Annie. They have been part of my book journey for as long as I've known them.

And to my husband, Joe, who has always encouraged me in every endeavor I've ever undertaken. We have had an amazing adventure in this marriage of almost fifty years. I loved you from the start.

PHOTOGRAPH CREDITS

Page 1: Official White House Photo by Adam Schultz
Page 2, photos 1–3: Photo by Adam Schultz / Biden for President
Page 2, photo 4: Official White House Photo by Adam Schultz
Page 3, photo 1: Lelanie Foster / *Real Simple*
Page 3, photo 2: Courtesy of Mark D. Sikes
Page 3, photo 3: Official White House Photo by Cameron Smith
Page 4, photo 1: Official White House Photo by Cameron Smith
Page 4, photos 2–4: Official White House Photo by Erin Scott
Page 5, photo 1: Official White House Photo by Adam Schultz
Page 5, photo 2: Courtesy of the Biden Family
Page 6, photos 1 and 2: Official White House Photo by Erin Scott
Page 6, photo 3: Courtesy of the Biden Family
Page 7, photos 1 and 3: Official White House Photo by Erin Scott
Page 7, photo 2: Official White House Photo by Abe McNatt
Page 8, photo 1: © Annie Leibovitz
Page 8, photos 2 and 3: Courtesy of the Biden Family
Page 9, photo 1: Official White House Photo by Adam Schultz
Page 9, photos 2 and 3: Courtesy of the Biden Family
Page 10, photos 1 and 3: Official White House Photo by Adam Schultz

Page 10, photo 2: Courtesy of the Biden Family

Page 11, photos 1–4: Courtesy of the Biden Family

Page 12, photos 1–3: Official White House Photo by Erin Scott

Page 12, photo 4: Official White House Photo by Adam Schultz

Page 13, photos 1 and 3: Official White House Photo by Erin Scott

Page 13, photo 2: Official White House Photo by Adam Schultz

Page 14, photo 1: Courtesy of the Biden Family

Page 14, photos 2 and 3: David Lienemann / Biden for President

Page 15, photo 1: DOMINIC GWINN / Middle East Images / AFP via Getty Images

Page 15, photos 2 and 3: Official White House Photo by Adam Schultz

Page 16: © Annie Leibovitz

ABOUT THE AUTHOR

Jill Biden, former First Lady of the United States, is the *New York Times* bestselling author of *Where the Light Enters* and her children's books *Don't Forget, God Bless Our Troops*, *Joey: The Story of Joe Biden*, and *Willow the White House Cat*. She served as Second Lady of the United States from 2009 to 2017. During the Obama-Biden administration and as First Lady, she advocated for military families, the Biden Cancer Moonshot, community colleges, and women's health research—and maintained a full-time career teaching English as a community college professor. She chairs the Milken Institute's Women's Health Network. A mother and grandmother—and now great-grandmother—she lives with her husband, former President Joe Biden, in Wilmington, Delaware, with their cat, Willow.